The Poetic Art of

WILLIAM BUTLER YEATS

FREDERICK UNGAR PUBLISHING CO.

New York

The Poetic Art of

WILLIAM
BUTLER
YEATS

ROBERT BEUM

This book could not have been written without
the encouragement and guidance of
Francis Lee Utley and the lucid
metrical studies of Paul Fussell, Jr.

Preface

However minute the employment may appear, of analyzing
lines into syllables, and whatever ridicule may be
incurred by a solemn deliberation upon accents and pauses,
it is certain, that without this petty knowledge no man
can be a poet; and that from the proper disposition of
single sounds results that harmony that adds force to
reason, and gives grace to sublimity; that shackles
attention, and governs passions.

—Samuel Johnson

THE DEVELOPMENT of a great poet's art is always a fascinating
story; and a necessary part of that development is the poet's
discovery and mastery of the metrical forms that will allow
his individual genius its fruition. Whatever others may believe
about the writing of poems, the poet himself knows only too
well how crucial a matter prosody is. Sensitivity, ambition, a
love of words, a store of impressions, experiences, and convictions—all this and more may be granted: it is the endowment of many people who never become poets and of many
poets who seldom or never rise to excellence. The ultimate
problem lies elsewhere. What the poet must find, in the very
process of forging his style, is propitious forms: forms congenial to his own temper and architectonic ability, forms that
will not run against the grain of the mother tongue, forms
that have not yet been exhausted by generations of brilliant
achievement or made untenable by changes in sensibility and
language.

Of course, poetry can to some degree refuse to bother with rhythm and sound and still be partly—though only partly—successful : witness much modern poetry of the "realist" sort, in which metrical considerations are wholly abandoned and only novelty or "problems" or striking imagery or a sense of urgency or raw power are deemed necessary. But the point is that such poetry—which sacrifices, whether from mistaken aesthetic doctrine or sheer ignorance or willful perversity, the complete matching of sound and sense at every point—does present the imagination with an ultimately imperfect pleasure. Even a writer of prose, if he hopes to wear well, can by no means afford to be heedless of the physical qualities of his medium; with a poet it is a crucial matter. So is the study of the physical texture a crucial matter for anyone who wants to understand verse as an art.

As a result of the psychological bias of modern criticism and of the steady decline of rhetoric as a formal study in the schools, prosody is usually slighted today; in the universities one meets professors of English literature who are unable to scan a heroic couplet or say whether a meter is trochaic or iambic. But a scrutiny of rhymes and meters can be fully as absorbing and rewarding as the pursuit of ironies and archetypal patterns. To see a poet searching for adequate metrical forms, to see him advancing in metrical technique as in vision, adapting his verse to the changing shapes of his spirit, and finding at last, perhaps after a great deal of uncertainty and anguish, a form that results in some great English poetry —what can be more compelling? Browning, after minor success with lyric pieces and failure with plays, hit at last upon the dramatic monologue in pentameter verse, a thing perfectly suited to his temperament and previous practice; Byron, neither disciplined nor genuinely romantic enough for those early Spenserian stanzas, opened up his richest vein with a newly discovered *ottava rima*, a roomy and rather elaborate stanza which, paradoxically, he had been somewhat prepared to handle by the false start of the Spenserians.

My own interest in Yeats's metrics began in a most unscholarly way : it started with my admiration for those many octave poems of his whose textures seemed to me, as they have seemed to many others, the mellowest and the most resonant in both sound and sense since the late odes of Keats. Here was a magnificent achievement. How did it come about? In his early poems Yeats was characteristically a poet of quatrains; in his middle and later years, these octaves, again and again. How did four lines prepare him for eight? Then one question followed another. Why did Yeats take up a form— the *ottava rima*—that seems unusually difficult in the English language and that had lain almost unused for a century? And who provided his models, or were there any? Why is there so little blank verse (outside the plays) and no free verse, always rhyme and so much slant rhyme? I felt that in trying to answer questions such as these I would learn more about Yeats the artist and Yeats the man. I thought that one might learn some things that would enlarge our understanding of some of his attitudes and intentions and that such a study would give us a clearer picture than we now have of his development as a master of English verse. One thing, at least, was certain : Yeats's rhetoric and symbolism, as well as his rather dramatic life, had proved so fascinating that we had overlooked the significance of his metrical art.

In the present book I have set out to describe that art and to discover its rationale. In attempting to do so I have naturally sought to gain principle and perspective by determining how Yeats's practice fits into the traditions of English prosody. It is only within the context of the whole tradition that an individual poet's metrical art can be seen clearly and in something like its full significance. Being a great poet who was also prolific and fairly eclectic in prosody as in genre, Yeats in turn, of course, enables us to see more clearly certain tendencies and patterns within the tradition itself. This book, looked at one way, is in fact as much about the English metrical tradition as it is about Yeats.

I have said that I hoped, from the outset, that a close study of the prosody would help to refine the image of Yeats that has formed over the years. That image is certainly not distinct in all aspects : there is still, even among the most careful and least polemical of the critics, dispute about Yeats's temperament and beliefs. Much analysis of his themes and images and mythic systems is now on hand; it needs to be supplemented by a scrutiny of the versification.

At the same time I should not be misunderstood as trying to deduce the subtleties of Yeats's heart and mind from a study of his metrics merely to present a new or more accurate biographical image. I am not trying to write biography, and I am not qualified to write on psychology (indeed very few psychologists seem to me qualified to do so). Trying to define some of the ways in which the prosody expresses the man's tastes or values need not lead us away from the poems themselves and into extraliterary speculations. The work, the artifact, is the proper sphere for literary appreciation and critical evaluation. Like all good poets Yeats converts his vision and his values into new, unique verbal structures, the originally proposed matter sometimes undergoing in the process a very considerable metamorphosis and much depersonalizing—even in a poet who is essentially an autobiographical Romantic; and it is this new creation, not the matter or conditions that preceded it, with which the reader must be primarily concerned. Closer definition of Yeats's values and leanings is desirable in its own right, but its chief value is to make possible more accurate and more comprehensive literary appreciation. Yeats is sometimes a particularly difficult poet : all avenues are worth exploring.

My treatment is not, I trust, merely impressionistic. However it is, on the whole, somewhat informal, and it is far from exhaustive. A more technical book might well be useful; I simply have not cared to write one myself. I want to maintain a certain breadth of view, to stick to what I take to be the more significant and problematical aspects of Yeats's prosody. I confess to having developed over the years a measure of respect for the traditional—that is, informal—sort of literary inquiry (the sort often written, in fact, by Yeats himself). My tolerance of imprecision or fuzziness is, I hope, as little as the next man's; but far be it from me to encourage the current vogue, which might be called "jargon with statistics." Surely there is something to be said for keeping stipulative terms and charts and tables to a minimum and small points in perspective. Neither clarity nor accuracy is an innovation that had to wait for the computers, the literary scientists, and the neologists. And it seems particularly incongruous to subject the *technē*-hating Yeats to their methods.

With the verse of Yeats's early poetry I have dealt only summarily. The early poetry (with a few magnificent exceptions) amounts to little more than apprentice work for the later. Consequently the proper focus of any study that takes the whole body of the poetry in view is upon the work Yeats produced from about 1910 onward. The earlier poems are not only less interesting and consequently less of an invitation to extended discussion; they are also written, on the whole, in late-Victorian measures with which everyone is already perfectly familiar, whereas the later work presents innovations that plead for comprehension and appreciation. The opinion still sometimes advanced that Yeats's early poetry is on the whole superior to the later is surely mistaken. Its only real use is as a defense against that horde of modernist depth-hunters who are attracted to the complex later work of Yeats largely because it offers excellent opportunities for ingenious explication and for resting serenely in an easy equation of modernity with excellence. In any case the poems Yeats wrote between 1880 and 1909 or so are no more superior to his later poems than Keats's verse of 1816 is superior to the odes of 1819.

Nietzsche said that the greatest evidence for the freedom of the will lies in the fact that occasionally someone comes along who is daring enough to challenge the doctrine. My own taste happens to be unfashionably conservative, and so I would be happy to be able to arrive at a more favorable judgment on Yeats's more obviously traditional, more "poetic" work. The Irish poet's now undeservedly unread friend Robert Bridges got worse as he got more modern and experimental (this, incidentally, may be the only judgment on which T. S. Eliot and Yvor Winters ever agreed). Not all men improve with the years; but Yeats was one of those who did.

I have given Yeats's plays rather short shrift, and the reader may well wonder why I bothered to include this chapter at all. I did, in fact, seriously consider omitting all mention of the plays, which are really outside the scope of the present book. However, I saw that my analysis of the metrical art of the poems—and particularly the generalizations that I drew from the analysis—could not but be seriously weakened without at least a cursory look at the plays. My chapter is nothing more than a supporting suggestion which proved, however, too lengthy to be cast as a note or appendix.

One omission I feel compelled to explain. I have offered nothing on Yeats's possible debt to Gaelic poetry or music. T. R. Henn has suggested in his study of Yeats, *The Lonely Tower*, that a really thorough study of the poet would need to investigate such a possibility. I can only think that the inquiry, however tactful and patient, would prove unusually barren. It is difficult to believe that Yeats's poetry shows any prosodic influence whatever from Irish song and verse. My own musical training is sparse, and I know little Gaelic. But in any case the facts are that Yeats himself was no linguist, never learned Gaelic, never made any particular study of Gaelic verse, seldom heard it recited, and had notoriously little ear for or love of Euterpe's art as practiced in Ireland or elsewhere. The music of verse was all his music, and it was English verse. His measures and stanza-forms are as typically English as Hardy's, Blake's, or Swift's. Tetrameter and pentameter quatrains and sestets, all end-rhymed and iambic —straight from Albion! The scholar who will pursue Yeats's Gaelicism undiscountenanced by such negatives has more leisure than I.

Finally I should say that I have presupposed a reader who is familiar with the more fundamental concepts and developments in English prosody or at least a reader who is willing to increase his knowledge in that area in order to understand Yeats better. At the same time I have tried to write in such a way as to avoid prosodic dogmatism and minimize the possibilities of relatively fruitless quibbling. There are "schools" in prosody, as in everything else, and one must ultimately take a stand somewhere; but it is more important to see the larger metrical issues than to wrangle over the finer points of scansion or terminology.

As for the mechanics of my scansion in the present book : a dot (·) designates a nonstress, a slanted bar (/) a primary stress, and two slanted bars (/ /) a secondary stress.

R. B.

November 1968

Charlottetown, Prince Edward Island

Acknowledgments

PARTS OF THIS BOOK were originally published as essays in the *Michigan Quarterly Review* (Ann Arbor), *Papers on English Language & Literature* (Southern Illinois University at Alton), and *Texas Studies in Literature and Language* (Austin). I wish to thank the editors of these journals for granting me permission to adapt the essays to the needs of the present book. For permission to quote from the works of W. B. Yeats, I am grateful to The Macmillan Company, New York.

Contents

1

Each Single Pace

. . . Poetry, with rule and order strange,
So curiously doth move each single pace
As all is marred if she one foot misplace.
—Sir John Davies, *Orchestra* (1596)

YEATS would have appreciated Davies's lines: they imply a view of poetry that can only be called the traditional view, a view that has prevailed not only in England and Ireland but at all the round earth's imagined corners, a view rarely challenged until recent times—times, interestingly enough, of massive intellectual confusion and social fragmentation. It is a view that has accommodated poets as different as Jonson and Keats, Chaucer and Shelley, Vergil and Milton, Camoëns and Sung Yü. One must get it in plain sight or not see Yeats in the right perspective.

What is poetry? To keep my discussion proportionate and to avoid making a survey of theories and opinions that have long since inspired tedious successions of surveys, I shall adopt

1

a laconic strategy that is partly a direct confrontation of the question and partly an elaborate paraphrase of what are at once the most persistent and the most sensible answers that have been formulated or intimated. Poetry itself is the best authority on what poetry is. And to look at our three thousand years of poetry is to see at once that, compared with prose, poetry is relatively more difficult to write and comprehend, more intense, and more patterned.

Ezra Pound's now famous remark that poets should not be satisfied with anything less than poetry which is at least as well written as prose is an amusing irony that will help prevent us from saying thoughtlessly that poetry is a more difficult art than "that other Harmony." Pound had in mind the sloppy, sentimental versifying perpetrated by lovers of the worst in Tennyson and Wordsworth, and the top-of-the-head poetry, written by habit and formula, of which Southey was perhaps Britain's supreme example before the advent of *vers libre*. We are, of course, speaking of the relatively greater diffi-culty of composing (and fully understanding) excellent poetry than excellent prose. Even in times when poetry was ubiquitous and immensely prestigious, as in the heroic age of Greece (and for a while after) and the bardic age of Ireland, it presented obstacles nonexistent to the prose writer, and the latter faced in his own medium none of comparable difficulty. Keats's remark that poetry should come about as naturally as the leaves on a tree has misled a few people. He meant that to do one's best work one must, first, be a poet by temper and, second, undertake on each occasion of composition themes, genres, and idioms congenial to one's particular sensibility and strength. Keats's worksheets show us that his poems took as long to come naturally as the summer leaves that budded in April. Byron's charming carelessness in *Don Juan* required much care. Jonson's conviction that in moving slowly he was moving in the Muse's own time is well known. Milton, accept-ing the myth of Shakespeare's wondrous facility, was dismayed at the snail's pace of his own composition; if he had seen some of the Bard's drafts, he might have been heartened. There can be no doubt that ideal conditions occasionally come about

—as they probably did again and again, in fact, with Shakespeare and Marlowe—and produce an astonishing quantity of fine poetry in a short time. Yet a Balzac or a Dickens, writing in prose, leaves a Shakespeare and even a Southey far behind. A poet's voice is that of Arnold, who says credibly that one reason he abandoned poetry was that in order to write it he had to tear himself apart; and that of Yeats himself, who often spoke of the "devil of a lot of trouble" it cost him to cast his material into verse, of the agony of working all day and producing nothing final, or merely a sequence of four or five completed lines.

About the intensity of poetry, testimony is no less universal; to mention the point is almost to belabor it. A linguistically emphatic or dramatic quality—this is our first impression and our first expectation of poetry. The nature of this intensity is, of course, not widely understood, and will be a subject of inquiry in the present discussion.

No less obvious and no less important is the fact that practically all poetry has been written as verse, that is, in a distinct metrical pattern. Unlike prose, poetry is measured and usually symmetrical in many ways. Its sentences are measured into lines; its lines may be (and usually are) further measured into more or less regular alternations of "short" and "long," of "unstressed" and "stressed" syllables; and of course a number of other patterns may be and very often are built into the structure. Both modern "free verse" and Old Testament poetry are essentially unmetrical; both, however, do make use of the line, and the Old Testament poetry is also highly patterned by repetitions of words and images and by various techniques of rhetorical parallelism; free verse, too, sometimes shows such a symmetrifying principle and sometimes even establishes a rhythm almost metrical.

An intense pattern difficult to create and rich in meaning and effect—if men wrote in this manner, perpetuated this mode for thousands of years, it is a safe assumption that they found something appealing in it. However they may have delighted in silence, in speech, and in prose, they must also have delighted in shaping language in such a way as to engage the whole personality deeply. Persian and Greek, Jew and Arab, Roman and Carthaginian alike set their hearts on building a difficult artifact that would enable them to achieve an unusually great control over the way their language registered on the sensibility of reader or listener and that would have an impact which is roughly described by words such as intense, dramatic, striking.

We have been asking poetry itself what it is. What the critical tradition says most often is that the aim of poetry (as of imaginative writing generally) is first of all to produce pleasure. Both the Ancients and the sons of the Renaissance prescribed pleasure and excitement (overlapping categories, to be sure) as the immediate if not the sole aims of the purer, that is, least utilitarian, sort of poetry. Even the Middle Ages recognized that poetry *qua* poetry should give pleasure : the pleasure was, in fact, the sugar that made the moral medicine go down sweetly.

Classical doctrine is more romantic than many people realize. Again and again classical commentators say that poetry should be designed to create a response variously called admiration, wonder, enthrallment, transport. In the *Poetics* Aristotle constantly repeats that an effect of wonder is a requirement of tragic poetry; this emotion is as integral to his aesthetics as the "pity and terror" formula, which has become a tiresome oversimplification. "The element of the wonderful is required in tragedy" (xxiv.8). Incidents of the plot produce the best effect when they "come on us by surprise yet follow as cause and effect. . . . The tragic wonder will then be greater" (ix.11-12). His *Rhetoric* takes the same tack (viz. 1.2; iii.2) except that it makes wonder a desideratum of poetry in general. Longinus is bolder : "The object of poetry is to enthral," he says (*On the Sublime,* xv.2); and again : "The effect of poetic genius is not to persuade the audience, but rather to transport them out of themselves" (1.4). Horace requires a milder kind of pleasure : *dulcia*—charm, pleasantness; and *pulchra*—beauty or artistry of verse. In the Renaissance, Minturno and Castelvetro and Riccobono demand from poetry effects of *meraviglia* and *diletto*. In any case, since intellectual activity alone—sheer ratiocination, strict exposition of doctrine or fact—can scarcely be expected to generate any of these types of pleasure, it follows as a corollary that the main stuff, or at least an essential constituent of poetry, must be feeling and imagination. In other words, poetic discourse, whatever its cognitive or moral content, must set to work on the sensibility.

Now, in order to work vigorously on the sensibility, discourse must in some way disappoint our prose expectations, disengage itself from the willful and ratiocinative structures of ordinary discursive language. What today we call prose fiction disengages itself (for the most part) simply by content; poetry, a bolder art, makes a further disengagement. To move toward poetry is to move toward a verbal structure which offers a refined pleasure that results from our loving absorption in artistry and in the power of words to engage the sensibility as well as to make sense. The essential difference between poetry and prose is not, as popular naïveté and many dictionaries have it, a matter of specific emotional content, such as passionateness or sublimity, nor is it a matter of euphony. Many fine compositions universally acknowledged to be poems are neither passionate, sublime, nor euphonious. The one quality that all poetry, even inferior poetry, has and that no prose which remains prose ever has is a special sort of intensity. Prose is capable of very great intensity—even nonfiction prose, as witness some of D. H. Lawrence's essays or William Carlos Williams's "The Destruction of Tenochtitlan." But in poetry the intensity is also felt as a heightened vitality of the individual words and in fact of every aspect of the whole stream of sound they constitute. In poetry the words themselves and all their relationships with one another increase in solidity, sensitiveness, conspicuousness—call it what you will. Our wonderfully increased sensitivity to and fascination with the connotations and physical feel of the words and of the patterns they make—this is the essence of our experience of a poem. The increased conspicuousness of the individual words and of their semantic and prosodic relationships produces a corollary effect which, because of its high contrast with the kinetic impression prose produces, must be called *stasis:* you are moving backward in the poem at the same time that you are moving toward the final line, you feel the whole in the part. (Another corollary is that the heightened conspicuousness of every linguistic detail in a poem causes small awkwardnesses to make a great jar : "if she one foot misplace.") Prose is progressive, accumulative. In highly denotative prose—the purest sort—the words are a mere convenience, almost, in a way, a nuisance : one would glady dispense with them if the point, the datum toward which one is hastening, could be gotten in some more efficient manner (the purer sciences seek in fact to eliminate words insofar as is practicable). Modern poetic theory has long been unduly cowed by a relativism which constantly points out that poems differ markedly—in subject matter, imagery, diction, prosody, every way. Nevertheless all the poets from China to Peru have written a kind of discourse that is vastly different from ordinary prose—say, Francis Galton's or Thomas Hardy's—and distinctly different even from the poetic prose of Browne or Traherne. The common denominator of all types of poetry is the ostentation of the words, both in themselves and in their subtlest relationships with one another. This definition has the virtue of allowing one to call Shelley's little lament "Oh world! O life! O time!" a poem and still think it an inferior performance; it allows one to say that Milton's poems are poems and that the poems admired by the anti-Miltonists are also poems. Unlike anything to be found in Galton's *Hereditary Genius,* Shelley's composition has the qualities of stasis and verbal conspicuousness. Because the reader is unable to discover the source of the despair, which is simply sprung on him, the poem is obscure and sentimental and unable to move him. But it has the shape, the feel, of a poem—a poem it is.

We are compelled, I think, to conclude that the analysts who have figured language as having two dimensions—one practical, one imaginative—have not misled us. In its practical dimension language exists as a tool for searching out fact or inference and then for communicating the discoveries; it serves to make needs and desires known; it allows us to survive and to do a little better than that. But language is also an immense source of pleasure unconnected or at least not apparently or directly connected with will, appetite, or ratiocination. The mere power of utterance, mere articulation, gives pleasure even when it is directed to no material end. To go further, to be able to make a sound that is not only a sound but also produces an idea in the mind or a figure in the mind's eye—how delightful. Playful, or easy and euphonious utterances are another pleasure. To make formal or elaborate acoustic patterns—meter, alliteration, rhyme, stanza—is yet another. To bring into concord apparently dissimilar things— to call a weatherbeaten church seen from a distance "brown as owls"—is to do something both satisfying and unrelated to one's health or advancement. Ultimately, of course, this artistic or imaginative activity *is* useful, and Oscar Wilde's remark that "all art is quite useless" is quite useless. Aesthetic activity —saying a word for the word's sake, making a poem, or making a crazy metaphor because nothing seemed more natural at the moment—is useful because it satisfies human nature : it is useful, but not in the ordinary sense practical.

Probably, then, one should think of poetry as an area at one end of a continuum. At the one extreme is technical information and scientific theory, at the other *poésie pure*. Proceeding one way, you find that conception or information is everything; the faster you can grasp it, the better. The words are transparent; they register as ideas only. Going the other way, you find that the discourse begins to please by having just the words it does have and in that order. Language has begun to expand its aesthetic dimension. As you move further, into poetry itself, you find the words so chosen and so arranged that you must move forward circuitously. Even in swift-moving verse, like Homer's or Morris's, there is no rushing through the way you race across a paragraph of prose. Instead of moving right along one track, you move forward but you also move around—in the whorls of connotation— and back—to the knitting assonances and patterns of stress or quantity. At the extreme is "poetry which approaches the condition of music," the kind of poetry George Moore and others have sought, a poetry which is in essence the use of words purely for their evocative and "musical" pleasures. This is truly an art of fragments—of syllables, words, and phrases, not of sentences and the logical structures they make up. Words are reduced to their sheer phonology and to a phantasmagoria of connotations. The result is infinite ambiguity, an elusiveness that may be charming at times but is barely short of unintelligibility. It is an art that, striving for pure beauty, usually succeeds in achieving pure privacy or pretentious nonsense. In the poetry the world has agreed to call its best, it is not that theme, content, conception has disappeared; it is that the aesthetic potential of the words, both as they create an imaginative conception and as they exist in themselves and in their physical relationships with one another, has been intensely exploited. As you move through the stanzas of the *Faerie Queene* or the lines of Landor's epigrammatic lyrics, you are getting plenty of "message" but you are also being deeply engaged and pleased by the ostentation of the words and the now conspicuous larger and smaller patterns they create.

Consider the opening lines of D. H. Lawrence's free verse "Bavarian Gentians" (they happen to be vaguely iambic; the rest of the poem is quite "free"):

> Not every man has gentians in his house
> in Soft September, at slow, Sad Michaelmas.

The two lines form a nice contrast: the first might belong to prose; the second, unmistakably, is poetry. Your movement across the second line is vastly different from what it would be in the case of some such prosodic analogue as the following (which, let us suppose, is a fragment from an old legal deposition):

> On 6 September, at "Slow," said engine was . . .

Lawrence's line immediately "stops" you, starts leading you about and backward, as well as forward. "Soft September" is at once a curiosity; even the capitalization is unexpected. There is no such locution in ordinary prose or talk. It insists that you begin to feel and imagine—if you are ever to understand. The same with "slow, Sad Michaelmas." For ordinary purposes—expression of will or appetite, exposition of fact or theory—words just aren't put together that way. Now that they are, each has its own resonance, and you must give it individual attention. You are also forced to notice the alliteration of four initial *s*'s, in two pairs. Around you go, in the circuits of connotation, and back and forth, in the lacing of the sound correspondences. The alliteration furthers the effect of stasis; so do the prepositional phrases themselves : they are parallel in tone and conception and of about the same length. The net result of the choice and arrangement of the words is verbal conspicuousness and stasis, that is, *poetic* quality.

Such intensity seems unjustified unless it gives the impression of being the natural, the only possible language of an intense informing spirit. Language, after all, must serve the ends for which it is best suited; language, though it can—to some extent, and indirectly—"picture" and make "music," is *not* music or plastic art. The primary function of language is to communicate, particularly when the language is presented, made public. One looks for, one demands content. A notably impure poetry has been overwhelmingly preferred in all ages and nations, even by the poets themselves.

At the same time, poetry holds us because it is not merely ideas and perceptions. Good and great poetry is always wonderfully *tense* : on the one hand, it is about to turn into ideas and perceptions; on the other, it is about to become pure artistry. *Poésie pure* offers a much more limited experience. No doubt one reason why all but a little of the world's poetry has been written as verse is that meter is one of the easiest ways to help produce that tension or richness. Meter has the effect of adding to poetry an artistic, a planned, nonspontaneous element, although in itself meter is, in fact, both an artifice (we do not speak or think in meter) and something "natural" in some sense—regular rhythms abound in life, in the universe. The tension of metered poetry helps produce (other things being equal) a uniquely satisfying linguistic and imaginative experience. Whatever "raw power" it may be capable of generating, unmetered poetry, like poetic prose, is incapable of such an effect of richness.

Nevertheless it is necessary to emphasize the point that a formal prosody is not essential to poetry. Lawrence's "Bavarian Gentians" is, if imperfect, a poem of considerable merit, and so is the opening section of William Carlos Williams's free verse *Spring and All*. Ostentation of the stream of sound may be brought about by any number of means, as by unusual rhythm (e.g., meter), unusual pairing of words, unusual syntax, unusual collocations of sounds (rhyme, alliteration, assonance), by condensation, by cutting a unit of line across the larger unit of the sentence. A piece that does nothing of this sort will simply not be poetry (such a piece, for example, is Williams's "The Girl" : although presented typographically as poetry, the piece is prose and not even a particularly poetic prose). If this notion is valid (it is mine only by right of assimilation and extension from such articulators of the tradition as Coleridge, Charles Williams, and F. W. Bateson), then C. S. Lewis, for example, is probably wrong (in *The Allegory of Love* [1958], p. 319) when he says that Spenser's alliteration in the *Faerie Queene* is merely a "disease of the [Elizabethan] period." Together with the meter and rhyme of the Spenserian stanza, the alliteration exists as one means of making the language genuinely poetic—whether, on the whole, it succeeds is another question. All prosodic devices should be thought of as routes leading away from the logical, swiftly progressive domain of prose; they provide one way to shrink the practical dimension of language. They secure verbal conspicuousness, an increased attention for every part and aspect of the stream of sound; they act to interlace the parts, to bind them together in a unity like that of an organism, thus creating a sense of stasis, a phonological texture so rich that it forbids us, just as does the poem's semantic richness, to run the intellectual race of prose. Of course they also create, simultaneously, patterns and thereby the irresistible appeal of order :

1   2   3   3   1   2

As a *dare*=*g*ale *sky*lark *sc*anted in a *d*ull *c*age.

Let us have a final illustration. I have taken the view, which seems to me the traditional view, that poetry, as compared with imaginative prose, has undergone an enrichment; it has superimposed a verbal imaginativeness onto the imaginativeness of theme or conception. When the Redcross knight of the *Faerie Queene* peered into the monster Errour's cave

> his glistring armour made
> A litle glooming light, much like a shade.

The imaginative conception here consists, first of all, of the whole fiction of the characters and their episodes, of which this particular passage is one small part; more specifically, of the unusual yoking of gloom and light into a single image and concept. The verbal imaginativeness (and conspicuousness) is produced, in one way, by a richness of connotation so great as to draw our attention to the individual words—in the context of the poem as a whole, "glistring," "armour," "light," and "shade" have spiritual connotations as well as ordinary denotations; in another way, it is produced by the poet's having arranged the words in such a way as to create a relatively regular alternation of lighter and heavier stresses in an irregular but striking pattern of assonances and alliterations : notice the pairing of "glistring" with both "litle" and "glooming," "light" with "like," "made" with "shade," and the continuous texture of *r, l,* and *m* sounds. Poetic quality comes into existence when words are so chosen and so arranged as to form a verbal texture whose every feature becomes unusually conspicuous. In the sentence I am now writing, the physical qualities of the language pass almost unnoticed; they create intelligible sounds which in turn create ideation; the only important thing is to grasp the idea. But in Spenser's lines, or in Milton's vision of angels—

> In solemn troops, and sweet societies,
> That sing, and singing in their glory, move,

we find an experience—an unforgettable one that enlists the whole personality. This verbal intensity seems to me to be the common denominator of all the various types of compositions that, after the winnowing of generations, are still called poetry : verse and free verse, accentual and quantitative and syllabic poetry, rhyme and rhymelessness, epigram and epic, the work of Tennyson and T. S. Eliot, of Homer and Mallarmé.

Spenser and Milton were unimpaired by fuzzy doctrines of "self-expression," "throwing off the shackles," and "reflecting the age." To them, as to the ancients and the contemporaries who will be read again tomorrow, art meant first of all control and careful selection, and the art of poetry meant that one must attend to each single pace of the whole. Prose has its own requisites and makes its own valid appeal. But the man or woman who knows what poetry is and loves it, is a human being committed to a love of fine control, distinct pattern, concentration and intensity, and rich balance. This, I believe, is the heart of the ancient tradition that Yeats joyfully inherited.

2

Perfection of the Work

The intellect of man is forced to choose
Perfection of the life, or of the work. . . .
—Yeats, "The Choice"

SINCE the eighteenth century, ignorance of the tradition—and willful disregard for it or for certain aspects of it—has been fashionable, though poets who strike off the tradition have nothing to lose but their poetry. More importantly, poets have always differed markedly in their ability to follow where the tradition would lead, and this in itself explains why most of the poems produced in any age are bad or mediocre or at least flawed in various ways. We are all poetic, it may be; but few of us can become poets; and even if we do, few of our poems are likely to attain greatness or excellence. The odds are heavily against the conjunction, in one person, of so many talents (like strong empathy and verbal sensitivity and structural ability) and virtues of temperament (like tenacity and the ability to avoid or overcome distractions) and circum-

13

stances (like opportunities to be alone and at leisure, and the good fortune to survive modern education and modern society generally without becoming deracinated or hypercerebralized). Few people—least of all we Americans, who still have trouble shaking off the notion that sheer energy and an open heart can remove any obstacle whatever—realize how much is required to produce poetry the world will not willingly let die. All that can be predicted of an image-laden mind (like that of, say, Carl Sandburg or William Carlos Williams) is poetry that will seldom be lacking in concreteness. What of the other requisites? All that an ear for timbres and rhythms can guarantee is a poetry like Lanier's or Swinburne's—admirable as technique but (on the whole) boring as poetry because it is incompletely poetry. A fully successful poem is the absolute integration of all its parts and aspects. Poetry is not imagery, it is not metrical facility, it is not "raw power"; if it were, it would be much easier to write, and Sandburg, Swinburne, and Jeffers would be great poets (which, despite dust jackets and the listings and classifications of certain reference volumes, they are not).

Now prosodic excellence is partly a gift of verbal sensitivity (which, in certain respects, at least, is apparently as much a matter of genes as is musical aptitude) and partly an acquisition obtained through protracted and sometimes painful discipline—through trial and error and grateful submission to an arbiter of unerring taste (a type almost as rare as the potentially fine poet himself).

Ultimately what is required in terms of prosody is the ability to give perfect structure to a poem, that is, to give it a shape expressive of the experience with which the poem deals —and beyond that, to adjust, insofar as the language will allow, every particle of the structure so that its timbre and movement will help enact, or at least not contravene, the sense.

To take up the problem of construction first. The poet must bring the meter and the "meter-making argument" into correspondence, must proportion the number and the lengths of lines and stanzas or line groups to the nature and importance of the "content" of each successive stage of the poem's development. He must, for example, see to it that each image or conception in a series of closely parallel expressions receives an approximately (or exactly) equal number of words, feet, lines, or stanzas. He must learn to give a bipartite experience what it cries out for—two stanzas or distinct parts, not one or three, and to proportion the stanzas or line groups so that each makes a nearly equal contribution to the total conception. This logistical problem, which is simultaneously a matter of prosody and logic, every poet must face every time he starts a poem. And it is here, probably, that more poets fail than anywhere else. In any case, the interpenetration of prosodic and logical structure is decisive in poetry. Poetry is a temporal art, like music (and like prose), not a plastic art; it consists of sounds moving across time. One consequence of this fact is that a poem's chief sensuous impact on us as we read or hear it is the timbre and movement of those sounds. Another corollary is that not only the syllables but the larger units, the stanzas or stichic divisions themselves, are instinctively perceived in a time perspective : the number of stanzas a poem has must not be arbitrary, but expressive. One must be aesthetically and psychologically naïve (as many teachers and critics and some poets are) to suppose that the number of stanzas a poem has dare be arbitrary. Each white space between stanzas must either be expressive of some movement of thought or incident, or else it must repeat meaningfully (for emphasis or solidity) in, as it were, a new key the same motif developed in the preceding stanza.

The purpose of the present chapter is to demonstrate in a general way the crucial role of prosody in producing the goodly number of wholly and almost wholly satisfying poems Yeats was able to bequeath to us. My motive is chiefly simple curiosity : I want to know how Yeats obtains his effects and, ultimately, his excellence. Since he is in most ways a traditional poet, I may at the same time be able to discover some quite specific things about the art of English verse itself. I shall look at a very few of Yeats's poems, which I have selected largely on the basis of their being typical of his work as a whole. Proportion (and my own—and no doubt the reader's—endurance) dictates that I not take a greater number.

Suppose we look first at "To a Friend Whose Work Has Come to Nothing" (*Collected Poems,* p. 107), a poem often considered one of Yeats's best.

> Now all the truth is out,
> Be secret and take defeat
> From any brazen throat,
> For how can you compete,
> Being honour bred, with one
> Who, were it proved he lies,
> Were neither shamed in his own
> Nor in his neighbours' eyes?
> Bred to a harder thing
> Than Triumph, turn away
> And like a laughing string
> Whereon mad fingers play
> Amid a place of stone,
> Be secret and exult,
> Because of all things known
> That is most difficult.

Here is verse "up to date" in diction, tone, and over-all rhythmic effect without being self-consciously Modern, without soliciting the reader's automatic approval of Modernity. It could not have been written in 1610, 1740, or 1819; it is a modern poem, one which reveals that the writer has been awake to the tonalities of his own times, has put words and cadences together in a way his contemporaries will recognize as essentially "natural" in their day.

On the other hand, the poem makes us recall that the world does not start from scratch every day. There are traditions and conventions, many of them useful and admirable, some of them apparently indispensable; there are even verities, or whatever one wishes to call certain notions and values that persist in war as in peace, in temperate zone and tropic, in an urbanized no less than in an agrarian world. Yeats's poem is traditional : it is in rapport with this steadiness, it retains an over-all shape evolved in the past—it has coherence, classically argumentative structure, meter, rhyme, symmetry. In short, the poem is rooted but has new leaves. It creates an effect of richness, complexity, synthesis—an effect which, readers find, wears well.

This is only one aspect of the balance or tension Yeats, as a traditional poet, strives for. "To a Friend" is poised between the ordinary and the formal and memorable, between conversation and incantation. The diction is that of usual speech; only one word out of six and a half dozen has more than two syllables. There are few syntactical inversions, none of an extreme sort. Also the lines frequently run over; this diminishes aesthetic distance by decreasing, without destroying, the conspicuousness of a nonspontaneous, nonconversational unit, the line. The meter is far from rigid : to take only three examples, the second line contains an extra syllable (the last syllable of "secret"); the ninth and sixteenth lines begin with a stressed syllable, or inverted foot; the fifteenth contains a succession of three monosyllables ("all thíngs knówn") each of which demands a firm stress. Even some of the rhyme is irregular ("out" / "throat"; "one" / "own").

In all these respects, the poem moves in the direction of ordinary speech, of "realism." But other forces are at work pulling the poem in the opposite direction. First, there is the over-all coherence and eloquence, qualities not characteristic of ordinary speech (particularly in our day). There is the well-planned, imaginative simile, and there are occasional words or constructions not found in conversation or colloquial prose : "Whereon" is a formal, rhetorical word; "Triumph" shows old-fashioned capitalization; "neither . . . nor " is very formal. The line, a structure unknown in speech or prose, exists here, its integrity maintained, despite the frequent enjambment, by end rhyme and by Yeats's causing the ends of lines to correspond with the ends of clause or phrase groups, so that one is conscious of a slight pause even at enjambments. Finally the iambic meter, though not perfectly regular, is very distinct. The poem attains Yeats's goal of "idealized speech," a matter we shall look at more closely in a later chapter.

Still another aspect of the poem's balance is its harmonization of strong feeling on the one hand and judgment and control on the other. What all intense discourse should seek, says Coleridge, is the balance and reconciliation "of a more than usual state of emotion with more than usual order; judgment ever awake and steady self-possession with enthusiasm and feeling profound or vehement." Similarly "To a Friend" balances emotions and motive. The cause of the speaker's intensity is not obscure, and its effect not sentimental: the poem is not a mere outcry. Yeats has the courtesy to think of the reader, to take the trouble to explain—to imply clearly is a more accurate phrase—the background or context of the feeling so that the reader can enter into it.

Like every good poem "To a Friend" achieves unusual intensity, a tautness that is the product of its high feeling and of general rhetorical efficiency. It starts with the always emphatic and evocative word "Now," plunging us into Time and dramatic present time. The drama thus begun is not let down: we move at once into the confident (hence dramatic) tone of a man sure of his ground and at the same time into the drama of confrontation, direct address. As for that verbal intensity or conspicuousness which I have called the common denominator of poetry the world around, neither I nor any other commentator can demonstrate it satisfactorily. All the techniques and conventions poetry has acquired (and its readers learned) contribute to produce the quality. Certainly meter plays no small part. The metrical ictus usually coincides with the rhetorically more important monosyllables, thereby reinforcing their prominence ("For *how* can *you* compete"). The very fact that in verse the individual words are so juxtaposed as to form what they almost never (and never effectively for any length) form in speech or prose, a relatively regular beat, probably makes us more than usually alert to the connotations and physical qualities of the individual syllables and words themselves. Also, of course, words at the ends of lines secure additional conspicuousness from their rhetorically prominent position—and often, as here, from rhyme and pause as well.

Finally there is the question of sound matching sense. I do

not propose an exhaustive analysis, but will simply sketch a few patterns which the reader himself can augment at will.

When I first decided it would be feasible to use this particular poem as an example of the artistry of the mature Yeats, I did not realize that it would also allow me to make what must be considered a most important, though seldom articulated, point about Yeats's poetry in general. It is this: though Yeats has in fact conjured up some of the most striking and memorable imagery in modern poetry, he is on the whole very little of a descriptive poet. Yeats is not image after image, like Keats or D. H. Lawrence, nor one lyrical vignette after another, like Dylan Thomas. You will not go to the *Collected Poems* to listen to waterfalls or the slither and hiss of snakes enacted in timbre and rhythm. He is a stranger to the brazenly onomatopoeic Hopkins. His constant tendency is to make his poems concrete and dramatic not by sound-painting or the massing of images but by isolating some dramatic moment—a confrontation of parties or a crucial movement of the mind—as his subject. He almost always moves immediately out of the sensuous and onto some plane of generality derivable from it. This technique is the expression of a philosophical bent, a sort of Platonism of temper. Yeats is as full of "sentences" as the Elizabethan drama. For all his celebration of the sensuous—vivacious blood, fine horse or hound or bird, Ledean body—no force presses him more relentlessly than the passion to phrase the great commonplaces in such a succinct and eloquent form that no one who reads him can ever forget those capping lines and the values they carry.

I bring this up because it seems to me to explain the fact that there is never much to find when one goes through Yeat's poetry looking for onomatopoeia or other striking acoustic effects. A certain neutrality and normality prevails. His temper saves him from strain and pretentiousness. And it may not be wholly a question of temper. The influence of the tradition would bid a poet follow the same direction. Certainly our better poets have, in their maturity, shown little interest in obtrusive sound effects and have pursued image and description not for their own sake but as ways into the evocatively typical or philosophical. A Poe is a freak, and a Hopkins (when he is not freakish himself) depends for his success on a surrounding tradition of normalcy and quietness that makes him "fresh" and "vigorous." Wilde's scene-for-scene's-sake "Impressions" are a heresy and a dull one. Generally our poets have found their heart's desire a poem that is, above all, memorable, a poem one can live with in age as in youth; and they have seen that memorableness depends not on what many talented and earnest recent poets have given up—ingenuities of phrase, spectacles of sound-painting, subtle brilliances of imagery, bizarre associations from the "unconscious"—but on the paradoxical richness produced by great intensity integrated with great quietness or plainness, and on a certain simplification or succinctness that reduces all to point and essence, to myth, incantation, eloquence. Yeats, like other fine traditional poets, remembered the durable appeal of profound simplicity; he saw that a poetry of acutely observed and vividly limned particulars, or of virtuoso "music," is ultimately a less satisfying, less noble one than that which remembers the power that can be generated by large conception—the power of eloquent summary and of painful verity.

Again "To a Friend" is typical. Over-all there is a certain harshness or at least "masculinity" of sound. No effort is made to eliminate the awkward abutting of consonants (as in the *k-d* series of "take defeat") or actual hiatus of consonants (as in "ow*n*" / "*N*or" and "Bre*d to*"). There is a high incidence of the consonants (like *d* and *t*) usually considered less than euphonious. And of course all this tendency toward roughness is perfectly appropriate to the firm, alert tone of the poem. Yet it is not obtrusive : no one would call the poem an exercise in apt harshness. Similarly the rhyme sounds are generally heavy, made up frequently of long vowels, diphthongs, and the more sonorous consonants. And this, too, no doubt contributes appropriately to the firm tone of the speaker's exhortation : quietly effective, though again nothing spectacular.

Finally one might notice the matching of tempo and sense in lines 9–13. Four successive enjambments help—but again

quietly—enact the meaning : rapidity complements the movement into a gay, triumphant tone.

The speed produced by the running over of the lines is
reinforced by absence of internal punctuation and by the
concurrence of several short vowel sounds and short syllables
generally, as "a"—repeated three times—and "Amïd" and
"ănd" and "măd."

On the facing page of the *Collected Poems* is "September
1913," another poem occasioned by the controversy between
Yeats and the enemies of Hugh Lane.

> What need you, being come to sense,
> But fumble in a greasy till
> And add the halfpence to the pence
> And prayer to shivering prayer, until
> You have dried the marrow from the bone?
> For men were born to pray and save:
> Romantic Ireland's dead and gone,
> It's with O'Leary in the grave.
>
> Yet they were of a different kind,
> The names that stilled your childish play,
> They have gone about the world like wind,
> But little time had they to pray
> For whom the hangman's rope was spun,
> And what, God help us, could they save?
> Romantic Ireland's dead and gone.
> It's with O'Leary in the grave.
>
> Was it for this the wild geese spread
> The grey wing upon every tide;
> For this that all that blood was shed,
> For this Edward Fitzgerald died,
> And Robert Emmet and Wolfe Tone,
> All that delirium of the brave?
> Romantic Ireland's dead and gone,
> It's with O'Leary in the grave.
>
> Yet could we turn the years again,
> And call those exiles as they were

> In all their loneliness and pain,
> You'd cry, 'Some woman's yellow hair
> Has maddened every mother's son':
> They weighed so lightly what they gave.
> But let them be, they're dead and gone,
> They're with O'Leary in the grave.

It lacks the universality of "To a Friend," where the occasion is so completely transcended that no limiting, local Irishisms remain; and its bitter mockery of the unromantic, unidealistic men unworthy of the revolutionaries who died for them works chiefly on one's critical spirit, does not reach as deeply into one as "To a Friend." Still it seems to me a poem of considerable merit. The mockery and indignation are flawlessly rendered and are harmonized with a strain of pathos; and the poem's topicality stands only a little in the way of a reader who does not happen to know the details of the Irish troubles or of John O'Leary's career—small-souled Irishmen who have betrayed an ideal are not essentially different from small-souled men who have steered a similar course elsewhere. The whole conception will reduce to the yet more universal, perennial antinomy of the dream and the reality. The poem's context clearly establishes a general identity for O'Leary, Tone, and the others, making footnotes unnecessary.

I have chosen this poem because it forms, in two ways, an illuminating prosodic contrast with its more famous neighbor on the facing page. The latter is presented as a continuous series of lines; "September 1913" is divided into symmetrical stanzas. The rhyme scheme is essentially the same in both poems: *abab*. Why are we given white space between the eight-line groups of the one poem, but not between the four-line groups of the other? Obviously because in both cases Yeats is trying to follow the traditional prescription that a poem's prosodic structure should coincide with or support its logical or conceptual structure. Our minds instinctively (and insistently) work in such a way that when we see (or hear) a poem broken into sections or units, we expect that some phase of the conception or "plot" will also be completed at that point. Where the stanza culminates, there the sense too should reach a resting point. If the line groups or stanzas fail to show this quasi-independent status, the white spaces between them seem arbitrary, irrelevant, and the poem, we feel, lacks genuine poetic structure. Many of the poems of William Carlos Williams (to take a poet who is often interesting and partly successful despite such shortcomings) show this misleading, nonexpressive use of line groups.

In "To a Friend" the unit of thought sometimes carries beyond the four-line rhyme unit. For example, both lines 4 and 5 deal with the unwiseness of the friend's lowering herself by arguing with vulgar attackers. Similarly lines 12 and 13 constitute the continuous development of a simile. Yeats wisely prints the poem as a single unit. The rhyme units in this poem are not intended to support and coincide with the logical structure; rather rhyme is here utilized for several of its other well-known functions (Yeats's rhyming deserves a chapter of its own). But this is not quite the whole story. Closer examination reveals that the conceptual structure of the poem is bipartite : the first eight lines form a unit of thought that comes to a full stop at the end of a rhetorical question; the next eight lines constitute a logical bloc that closely parallels the thought of the first bloc (there are exact correspondences, even, as in the repetitions of "bred" and "Be secret"). The true structure, then, is that of two octaves logically parallel; the two rhyme units or quatrains within each octave are nonstructural.

Why not, then, print the poem as two stanzas instead of making it a continuous unit? Such a division could certainly be justified. Yeats may have felt that logically the two octaves were so much of a piece that typographical continuity would constitute the slightly superior presentation. There could be little quarrel, one way or the other.

The mere decision to adopt a refrain obligated Yeats to break "September 1913" into stanzas. But even if there had been no refrain, Yeats would have obtained an expressive deployment of stanzas : each stanza corresponds to a complete phase of the argument. The first octave is a mock endorse-

ment of the crass little men who give themselves wholly to
money and rote-said prayers : what else need they do, since
"Romantic Ireland's dead and gone"? The clearly logical
relationship of the second octave to the first is immediately
indicated by its opening word : "Yet." The reader can easily
discover for himself the logical justifications of the succeeding
stanzas and white spaces.

Later on in this book I shall be emphasizing Yeats's fondness for quatrains and octaves, the forms in which a large
majority of his most successful poems are cast. And so it may
be well here to notice his craftsmanship in the sestet, another
form he favors.

In "Who Goes with Fergus" we find an *abcabc* stanza in
which Yeats works more than a few times and more than a
few times succeeds.

> Who will go drive with Fergus now,
> And pierce the deep wood's woven shade,
> And dance upon the level shore?
> Young man, lift up your russet brow,
> And lift your tender eyelids, maid,
> And brood on hopes and fear no more.
>
> And no more turn aside and brood
> Upon love's bitter mystery;
> For Fergus rules the brazen cars,
> And rules the shadows of the wood,
> And the white breast of the dim sea
> And all dishevelled wandering stars.

Even in this early poem (a song from *The Countess Cathleen*)
Yeats achieves a solid construction, although its design is not
quite as perfect as that of "September 1913." The two sestet
stanzas are parallel in over-all conception : each is an image
of heroic joy, a Romantic's conception of primitive revelry
and identification with the natural world—qualities possible
before the development of abstract categories of thought
brought about our modern self-consciousness and loneliness,
our keen sense of being quite separate from nature. Each
stanza celebrates the abdicated poet-king's romantic domain

(the images of pleasure-chariots, woods, and seashore are repeated and in the same order in both stanzas); each cries encouragement to man and maid. But there still exists a certain structural imbalance : the opening line of the second stanza continues the thought and even the wording of the last line of the first stanza, and so a stanza break at that point can scarcely be justified. (Within the second stanza, the line grouping by rhymes is the balanced *abc* / *abc*; but the design of the thought here is an asymmetrical *ab* / *cabc*. By contrast the first stanza is internally balanced : three lines imaging and celebrating Fergus's free domain followed by three heartening man and maid. The second stanza is not necessarily flawed, however, for reasons we shall examine shortly.)

The much later poem "The Results of Thought" (1931) shows a firmer design in the same type of rhyming sestet.

> Acquaintance; companion;
> One dear brilliant woman;
> The best-endowed, the elect,
> All by their youth undone,
> All, all, by that inhuman
> Bitter glory wrecked.
>
> But I have straightened out
> Ruin, wreck and wrack;
> I toiled long years and at length
> Came to so deep a thought
> I can summon back
> All their wholesome strength.
>
> What images are these,
> That turn dull-eyed away,
> Or shift time's filthy load,
> Straighten aged knees,
> Hesitate or stay?
> What heads shake or nod?

In the opening stanza the speaker broods, in a tone that can only be called dark and regretful, on the wrecked spirits and bodies of his once beautiful and brilliant friends and loved ones. The second stanza brightens as the speaker's thought turns rather to his own ability, obtained after long discipline of thought, to recall, in a way that will actually invigorate him, "all their wholesome strength." And in the third and final stanza the speaker turns to look upon the friends and loved ones as if they had suddenly come into view. The poem's logical and stanzaic structures exactly coincide. Unfortunately the poem itself amounts to very little. It is marred by obscurity and personalism. The *I* is too much Yeats, too little everyman; and Yeats fails to make clear the nature of his power to revitalize himself, let alone intimate how we too may obtain this power. One must read *A Vision* (the "results of thought") in order to understand the three sestets very well; and in this case the result would not be worth the thought.

A far better sestet poem of the same scheme is "Her Anxiety," X of *Words for Music Perhaps*.

> Earth in beauty dressed
> Awaits returning spring.
> All true love must die,
> Alter at the best
> Into some lesser thing.
> *Prove that I lie.*
>
> Such body lovers have,
> Such exacting breath,
> That they touch or sigh.
> Every touch they give,
> Love is nearer death.
> *Prove that I lie.*

This poem, the utterance of an idealistic young woman confronting her beloved, expresses the poignance of the paradox that love is consumed in its own fruition. The first stanza centers around the mere fact (which the girl still hopes, of course, is not an inevitable fact) that love must die or at least diminish; the second focuses on the lovers, who in their ardency must either "touch or sigh" but who must find that "Every touch they give, / Love is nearer death." The poem shows Yeats's usual generalizing tendency and borders, in fact, on being barren and too conventional in diction. A sure fault exists in the poem's failure to make dramatic use of the image which opens the poem, that of earth awaiting returning spring; it is not in itself sufficiently developed for us to be at all sure how Yeats wants us to relate it to the girl's situation; nor does Yeats return to the image subsequently. The refrain, terse, vigorous, and tonally rich, does a great deal for the poem.

"Lullaby," XVI of *Words for Music Perhaps,* is perfectly structured : three stanzas, each of which develops an image of delicious sleep drawn from classical or romance mythology, and each of which shows about equal density of meaning.

> Beloved, may your sleep be sound
> That have found it where you fed.
> What were all the world's alarms
> To mighty Paris when he found
> Sleep upon a golden bed
> That first dawn in Helen's arms?
>
> Sleep, beloved, such a sleep
> As did that wild Tristram know
> When, the potion's work being done,
> Roe could run or doe could leap
> Under oak and beechen bough,
> Roe could leap or doe could run;
>
> Such a sleep and sound as fell
> Upon Eurotas' grassy bank
> When the holy bird, that there
> Accomplished his predestined will,
> From the limbs of Leda sank
> But not from her protecting care.

But again the poem is badly marred by stale diction ("mighty Paris," "grassy bank") or by diction inappropriate to the lullaby genre (Zeus, as the swan, "accomplished his predestined will").

Much more telling poems in the same verse form are "A Deep-Sworn Vow" and "On Being Asked for a War Poem."

The most interesting technical feature of the former, a moving poem which is rhetorically flawless, is not its sestet structure, but the great power generated by the unexpected rhyme of "face," the key word of the whole conception, with itself, and in its emphatic position as the last word of its line and of the poem itself.

I have never been able to formulate any ingenious guesses as to why Yeats favored the various sestet forms as much as he did. I must fall back on quite ordinary observations. For one thing, English poetry has produced far more stanzas with an even than with an odd number of lines, probably because the even number better accommodates effects of balance in thought. For another, six lines offer a bit more room than four, and a poet's conception sometimes needs the extra space. I am even tempted to guess that to some extent Yeats's initial reason for taking up some of his sestets was simply to get some relief from his perennial quatrains and compound quatrain schemes. As important as anything, no doubt, is the fact that in stanzas having an even number of lines each rhyme sound need be repeated only once—an important consideration in a rhyme-poor language like ours.

In other respects, as in that, the *abcabc* stanza (like its variants) offers no great difficulties. It is not by any means an elaborate stanza. And it allows, perhaps even encourages, the poet to move somewhat freely about instead of insisting that he toe the line of strict logical relationships. Since it seems natural to us that a rhyme scheme should approximately coincide with the thought scheme, it follows that in *abcabc*, where the rhyming lines are separated from one another rather than paired (as in a couplet or triplet), the very tightest logical relationships between the lines are not expected. In fact the sestet we are describing seems to arouse in the reader (or sensitive hearer) not the expectation of finding that the rhyming lines will mate logically in three pairs, but that the three contiguous nonrhyming lines will develop one phase of the thought and their three contiguous mates another. But the mere fact of the considerable separation of the rhyming lines seems to cause the reader to lose the thread of the form somewhat and therefore to build up no powerful expectations about the natural fulfillment of the form. More simply, what I am saying is that the stanza will feel all right to us (other things being equal) even though its logical structure does not match the rhyme structure in either the *aa / bb / cc* way or the *abc / abc* way.

If this hypothesis is correct, then we should expect to find two things in Yeats's sestets. First, that Yeats makes no consistent attempt to achieve within the stanza either the two-part or the three-part structure of thought. Second, that he seldom or never uses the *abcabc* sestet for his epigrams. We have already seen that he as often neglects as pursues the possibility of obtaining the internal logical balance. And when we look at Yeats's several epigrams, we see that almost all of them are cast in quatrain or couplet form, that is, in forms in which the design of the rhyme encourages tightness, quick balance, and mnemonic effect—qualities that define the genre. It is interesting to notice that in "On Being Asked for a War Poem," the one *abcabc* sestet that could reasonably be classed as an epigram, Yeats does build a balanced logical structure of *abc / abc*; and that in the few other sestet epigrams, such as "Swift's Epitaph," "On Those That Hated 'The Playboy of the Western World,'" and "A Drinking Song" (an epigrammatic lyric), the rhyme scheme of the stanza is such that it either brings the rhyme mates closer together, so as to obtain greater rapidity of effect and greater mnemonic power, or else repeats the rhyme sounds more than twice—in both cases the result is to obtain greater unity and intensity, more rapid effect, memorableness. The rhyme schemes of these three epigrams are respectively *ababcc, abacbc,* and *ababab.*

Again what is revealed is Yeats everywhere and always the prosodic artist, by instinct and conscious discipline seeking for each poem a form that will create the illusion that no other form would have done as well. His poems, like everyone else's, fail sometimes, on occasion quite badly; but they never fail because he believed that only a minimum of metrical artistry is needed to secure permanence for verse. Neither his ear nor his personality is perfect, and so he sometimes misses fire even prosodically; but he instinctively recognized that metrics is a crucial aspect of the poet's trade.

It is surely unnecessary to demonstrate that Yeats's standard practice is to end a line at the end of a natural phrase or clause. This is the habit of all traditional English verse, of poets as unlike as Milton and Skelton. If the best, not just a slipshod, poetry is to be aimed at, then the poet must make use of his line, which is one of several instruments at his disposal and one of the most basic. He can do this only by firming the line, by making it (over-all) clearly perceivable as a unit of composition. And to do this he must in turn do at least a minimum to make the line functional; otherwise it is merely an arbitrary piece of typography, or worse, the tacit advertising of something to be that which it is not.

Of the various devices available for marking the line so that it can function expressively, line termination at phrase or clause terminations is about the easiest (rhyme and end pause are others). Yeats follows the collective wisdom of his predecessors in this way as in others, and therefore he never writes in the pseudo lines that fill the anthologies of the New Poetry. Here are some lines I take from Yeats quite at random :

> (1) All things can tempt me from this craft of verse . . .

> (2) A cursing rogue with a merry face,
> A bundle of rags upon a crutch . . .

> (3) Those that I fight I do not hate . . .

> (4) I leave both faith and pride
> To young upstanding men
> Climbing the mountain-side . . .

> (5) Acquaintance; companion;
> One dear brilliant woman;
> The best-endowed, the elect,
> All by their youth undone,
> All, all, by that inhuman
> Bitter glory wrecked.

In every case but one the line consists of a complete clause or phrase (or phrases). The exception is line five of group 5 :

"inhuman" and "Bitter" belong in the same phrase. But notice that Yeats at least compensates for the conceptual runover by firming the line with rhyme; furthermore, the unexpected separation of normally contiguous words (only a traditional framework can make it unexpected) together with the place-ment of those words in positions of rhetorical prominence (at the end and beginning of lines) increases the emphasis on these words, an emphasis fully justified by their tonal importance.

A less successful instance of Yeats's departure from the traditional coincidence of line with phrase or clause meets one at the opening of the early poem "A Friend's Illness":

> Sickness brought me this
> Thought, in that scale of his:
> Why should I be dismayed
> Though flame had burned the whole
> World, as it were a coal,
> Now I have seen it weighed
> Against a soul?

The demonstrative pronoun "this" belongs with the word it points to even more strongly than is the case with the words in a sequence of adjectives and noun. Here the violation of naturalness is uncompensated. The effort to secure a rhyme has led only to strain. Neither "this" nor "his" can justify the emphasis it receives. The whole phrase "in that scale of his" is in fact unfortunate; it causes the sick friend to seem to possess the scale (of judgment) as if it belonged to him personally; in reality the scale is the speaker's—it may even be said to have existence independently of any particular man.

But I have had to hunt very diligently to find Yeats de-parting from the traditional structure of the line, and even more arduously to locate this one miscalculation. Never does he flippantly ignore the line, as, say, Thom Gunn does in the opening (and generally elsewhere) of "My Sad Captains":

> One by one they appear in
> the darkness: a few friends, and
> a few with historical
> names . . .

or as Robert Creeley does almost consistently in "The Name" :

> let my name
> be in you flesh
> I gave you
> in the act of
>
> loving your mother . . .

which gives us both psuedo lines and pseudo stanzas.

Finally I would like to suggest that yet another aspect of Yeats's adoption of a traditional art of verse (and therefore another reason for his permanence) is his avoidance of what may be called tyrannical meter. One axiom of poetics is that the meter of a poem—at least, of any poem longer than a few lines or stanzas and intended for the silent reader rather than for the chant of song of ritual—should not be absolutely regular. There are at least three reasons for this : first, rigid regularity tends to produce monotony; second, it allows the meter to ride roughshod over the other elements of the poem, producing an effect of imbalance, disharmony; third, it tends to create an impression of externality or what some recent critics call insincerity—the meter seems to be imposed upon the poem "from outside" rather than to develop organically out of the very subject, scope, and tone of the poem. This principle of obligatory variation is probably one of the chief reasons why English poets have so seldom undertaken (and never made a success of) a long (and serious) poem in trochaic meter—even though successful short poems in trochaic tetrameter abound. Trochaic meter is notoriously emphatic and at the same time difficult to vary without destroying. A piece which suffers from tyrannical meter is Tennyson's panegyric "To Virgil," which begins

Roman Virgil, thou that singest Ilion's lofty temples robed in fire
Ilion falling, Rome arising, wars, and filial faith, and Dido's pyre

In its twenty lines I fail to discover a single deviation from the percussion of the trochees. It is a tour de force; but is it a good poem? Tennyson, Browning and Swinburne are rife with this metrical imbalance, and one can only endorse the oft-heard suggestion that it is one reason for their decline (their futile attempt to make triple rhythms serve as the prosodic vehicle of serious English poetry is another). Yeats can be given, as I say, a clean bill of health on this particular score. Even the early poetry, which shows in so many ways (for example, in its hankering after the anapest) the influence of the Victorians, avoids the error. The fact that it does, seems to be evidence that Yeats possessed even at the outset of his career both an intuitive grasp of the necessity to keep all the elements of a poem in balance and an approach to poetry that was more the approach of a man of vision and strong feeling than that of a facile metrist or metrical dabbler. For emphasis I repeat a point I have made earlier : the most cursory study of the best poems English poets have written reveals that a fully satisfying poem is not rhythms—however "beautiful" or striking they may be—but the harmonization of rhythm, image, diction, conception, and all else. Yeats achieves this balance again and again, which is why even a man of the Left like Louis Macneice can say that as many as seventy or eighty of Yeats's poems are masterpieces.

As we shall continue to see throughout this study, Yeats consistently pays attention to even the smallest linguistic details : he is committed to striving for maximum control of his medium. The productions of many more recent poets compare quite unfavorably. Of many contemporary poems which have achieved a certain vogue, one can only say that though they are by no means devoid of art, neither are they products of ambitious artistry. They are artistic in that they sometimes show clarity, controlled tone, relative conciseness, etc. But no one will go to them to witness the great dance of Dionysus with Apollo, that dance so spellbinding because so rich and difficult. No one will find in them that old marriage of intricate design with imaginative freedom and strong feeling; nor will one find much delicacy of rhythm, or continuous delicate adjustments of sound and sense, or the mnemonic resonance of rhyme and assonance. The conception and the personal feeling of the writer have been made all-important. The reader gets one thing for his money; the old metrical poetry gave him two things : a theme or conception and, in de Selincourt's phrase, a revelation of beauty—"that which, when seen, is loved." The traditional poet's intense artistry, extending through each single pace of the whole, finely adjusting all things as the language allows, created a paradigm of absolute discipline, absolute control, absolute devotion to both conception and medium : the poem stood as a memento of all beauty, wakening in the reader or hearer an exaltation not unlike that fine catharsis at the end of *Hamlet* or *Samson Agonistes.* We have long been in danger of settling for a new poetry that will give us just feeling and idea and a minimal artistry. The most fashionable poetry today is a kind of art that is egoistic and close to autobiography. At its extreme, it does little more than seek to publicize its author : it seeks to convince the reader that the writer is a good modern liberal, *au courant.* It is not as easy to write this kind of poetry as its harshest critics suppose, but it comes easier—by a good measure—than interesting metrical poetry. Its relative easiness and modernity recommend it to the poet, the latter quality to the market, and so one finds it the preference, almost the dogma, of a good many magazines, lecture halls, and anthologies. It may satisfy various of our needs : some of it may be alert and unpretentious (though much of it is, in fact, quite pretentious) in a world that is not; in another sense, it may "capture the spirit of the times." But it is not a high artistic achievement, and it does not have the ring and the shine, therefore, of successful traditional verse. It may be "graphic" and powerful at times; it is not memorable; it does not change one's life, as Shakespeare and Keats and Yeats have changed it.

3

Prosody as Expression

Style is the image of character.
—Gibbon

Height of style is the echo of a great personality.
—Longinus

PROSODY, like any other aspect of a poet's work, is both a personal and a historical matter.[1] It relates the poet to his age —in the 1590's he will likely write sonnets and blank-verse plays, in the 1690's couplets for poems and plays alike—and at the same time identifies him as an individual, a man of particular strengths, limitations, and preferences, a man choosing this and rejecting that, and in any case revealing himself in everything he touches or refuses to touch. Pope's urbane couplets make him an Augustan; they also make him Pope: no one else uses the form in exactly the same way. "Language most shows a man : speak that I may see thee," says Jonson; and a poet speaks in the language of metrics. T. S. Eliot's

35

dictum that the genuine and mature artist seeks not to express personality but to escape from it by no means destroys the ground of the adage : style remains *in some way* the man. Of course *Le style, c'est l'homme même* is much more of a truism when the poet writes with what F. W. Bateson calls "sincerity," that is, when the poet is writing directly out of his own experience and dearest values, allowing the matter to evolve its own form. One can see more of Yeats in his prosody than one can see of Surrey in his for the simple reason that as an heir of the Romantic tradition Yeats believed in allowing his verbal artifact to be shaped (in the process of composition) quite directly and pervasively by his own unique experience and by his own ear and architectonic sense. Poets of the early Tudor period did not share our modern psychological and autobiographical obsessions. They were writing (I speak of the typical practice) to please a courtly, tradition-mindful audience by way of familiar themes incarnated in genres and verse forms also rather set (e.g., elaborate, euphonious, quite regular end-paused rhyming pentameter). They had, no doubt, as rich an inner life as their descendants, but consciously and unconsciously they were content to censor a wide range of thought and feeling—and the prosodic concomitants—out of their songs and sonnets, romances and verse letters, which are "built by the rules."

Certainly in modern times form and style reveal character and experience just as substance does : not always readily or with perfect reliability, and not to the depths of their mysteries, of course, but in some of their essentials nonetheless. Balzac (Yeats's favorite novelist) was deeply interested in his own personality and experience, yet possessed of powers of empathy as protean as Chaucer's or Shakespeare's; energetic and voraciously observant; fascinated by the historical spirit, by the panorama of an epoch, but also by the smallest details of objects, features, and processes of all sorts; generally exhilarated, rather than depressed or unnerved, by the motley and relativity of life; well-dabbled in many things, yet deep in several; in demeanor and habit rather coarse and awkward, in some ways quite sloppy or vulgar; devoted to woman and the Church; fascinated by money and contemptuous of materialism; world-wise and world-loving yet humble and spiritual; rather tough-minded and yet attracted by the romantic, the sentimental, the mystical. And there we have not only sketched the man but hinted strongly at the features of Balzacian prose. There is no great disparity between the man and the prose; *The Human Comedy* is in direct ways (and not only in *Louis Lambert* and *La Peau de Chagrin*) autobiography as well as objective drama.

Yeats himself talked more about the other kind of artist : the artist whose work embodies every quality the man himself seems to lack. In one of the most brilliant and amusing passages of *The Trembling of the Veil* (1922) Yeats takes up the figure of William Morris, a cheerful yet irritable and easily flustered man who chose to be dignified, delicate, and melancholy in his art. The case of Landor—a poet Yeats loved above most others and to whom he is indebted for resonance and epigrammatic strength—is similar : a volatile, irascible, perennially upset man, equable only with his dogs; yet whose work (that which lives) has become a byword for charm and serenity, both the verse and the prose having the quality of statuary.[2] What we lack, seek, admire from afar—nothing is more central to the personality.

We can expect to discover an expressive rationale in a poet's choice and handling of verse forms over a period of years, just as we can expect to see it in his genres and in his imagery. Most poets—most writers of every sort, for that matter—tend to keep working the same or much the same veins year after year, decade after decade. As a rule they launch out into something new—new for them, or in a few cases for anyone—only out of jadedness or changing critical or popular demand. Dickens goes on with his caricatures and gusto and sentiment, Conrad with his exotic and psychological prose romances, Yeats with his lyric-dramatic short poems and short lyric plays and short poetic familiar essays.

This is hardly esoteric doctrine. It is what we imply when we speak of a writer's finding himself.[3] He finds, at once or at last, genres and modes that answer to his own taste and to his own strengths in endowment and experience. A poet tries his hand at various things and discovers that for him certain prosodic forms come off better than others, just as he finds certain subjects and certain tonalities congenial to him personally. The ideal is to discover and then stick to the forms his unique bent and experience enables him to exploit with relative facility—at least, with strong intimations of ultimate success—and that will at the same time attract the sort of audience to whom he would like to make his appeal. Swift, living in an age that adored clarity and urbanity, found that he possessed a suave and lucid mind together with clear moral and aesthetic convictions—and consequently with a fund of irony and indignation. Exactly a century later Keats found a call to sensuous lyricism and poignant melancholy and romantic metrics, and he found, outside, a world that on the whole no longer proscribed such things and that in part was ready to acclaim them.

Even when the milieu strongly censures certain forms and strongly prescribes others, the poet will show his individuality. Anglo-Saxon poetry, despite its fixed versification, limited vocabulary, and habitual verbal formulas, is not of a piece. Being oneself is, after all, inevitable. In any age, a poet may choose to write as a rebel; but individuality inheres in nuances as in rebellions and stark contrasts. Most writers are content, on the whole, with the poetics of their era. They obtain their individuality simply by the particular directions and by the intensity of their application to their craft; or they may modify the prescribed genres and forms by taking advantage of whatever degree of deviation is tolerated. In a time when the pressure to write couplet satire was very great, Parnell and Smart went their own way. Thomson and Collins, a bit more deferent to orthodoxy, risked censure to accommodate their own romantic and odic biases. Goldsmith stuck with the couplet and with social verse, but he had to relax the former and soften the latter from pungent wit to genial humor. A poet's metrics begs to be explained from a personal viewpoint as well as from that of historical context; his prosody reflects taste and ability and need, just as his themes and

genres do; it is, in short, a record of experience. In looking at
the metrical forms a poet chooses—and of course at those he
avoids—and at his characteristic ways of working in them,
and at his successes and weaknesses, we are discovering something of his mind and heart. When the body of all other
evidence is not ample or not quite distinct, a study of the
prosody can be especially helpful in substantiating or modifying accumulated suppositions about the poet's values and
intentions and about the influences of other writers on his
work.

Thus Spenser looked back lovingly and indebtedly to
Chaucer and, insofar as he knew or imagined it, to the native
verse tradition generally. We know this, of course, from bits of
explicit praise here and there in the poetry; but we also feel
the indebtedness in the alliterative and accentual measures of
the *Shepheardes Calender* and in the ubiquitous rhyme-royal
stanzas of Spenser's middle period. It is the study of Spenser's
prosody, as of his themes and inconography, that enables us to
define his relationship to the older English tradition on the
one hand and to active, contemporary continental work on the
other. Why, for example, did he so seldom write in couplets
(a favorite of his master Chaucer and an "easy" form) and
never in blank verse (again, an easy form and one fashionable
in Spenser's day, though more for drama than for poetry)?
Or to take the question the other way around, why did he so
often insist upon the most elaborate verse forms? Because
artificyall was a good word to the Elizabethans? Yes; but also
because of the influence of Marot and of the Italian *canzone,*
and of the Middle English tradition of rhyme, derived from
the Normans; and also because Spenser loved ceremoniousness
and a sweet, reluctant, amorous delay too much to favor blank
verse or pentameter couplets. The last thing he wanted was a
plain or proselike form, or a pointed and packaging one that
would have been at odds with the diffusive rhetoric he employed to elevate his style.

It should be possible to refine our comprehension of both
Yeats the man and his metrics by looking for correlations between the two, and to do this without losing sight of the solider,

less speculative goal of describing his art of verse in general— its major features and the effects they create. To do less, to leave the larger implications of a great poet's prosody un- examined, is to take little risk—except that of contributing another fragment, another specimen of divorce and specializa- tion, to a world beginning to be appalled at the accumulation of such things, a world that cries out for synthesis and whole- ness, even for small steps in those directions.

4

Yeats's Mature Style

One's feelings lose poetic flow
Soon after twenty-seven or so.

THE ADAGE is probably truer of people in general than of poets in particular. Spenser wrote the *Epithalamion* and Shakespeare *The Tempest* in middle age; Landor and Bridges wrote great poems in their eighties. Keats's fine saying comes to mind to counter the popular notion : "Nothing is finer for the purposes of great productions than a very gradual ripening of the intellectual powers." In any event, flow is not everything, not even in poetry. Yeats gained little poetic *force* before forty-seven or so. He was about as far removed as it is possible to be from the poet of precocious genius or from the poet whose sensibility burns itself out quickly. In mature years he himself deprecated that "violent energy, which is like a fire of straw, consumes in a few minutes the nervous vitality, and is useless in the arts."[4] In his twenties Yeats's thought (as it

41

received expression in his poems, that is) was commonplace or hopelessly misty, his range limited, his imagination only conventionally poetic. Criticism has not gone wrong in regarding the early poetry as minor. At present it is unduly neglected, but the judgment is basically right. Yeats himself knew that his strength lay in the later poetry; he says so everywhere in his later prose and letters. Richard Ellmann, speaking of the two styles of the early verse—"folk" and "literary"—says rightly that "each style seems slightly contaminated by the other, as if he did not yet fully understand either,"[5] and Randall Jarrell put the matter when he said that "the most common subject of the poems is a passive, Platonic, and hopelessly unrequited love," and pointed out the "limp, wan rhythms, and enormous quantities of adjectives and intransitive verbs."[6] Up to about 1910 the verse is preoccupied with the idealized romantic past; it is full of vaguely poignant moods, vague thought and imagery, unexamined archaism and inverted word order, and fashionable melancholy. This is not to deny the beauty of individual lines and even of a few poems; the work is not as unengaging as moderns in quest of the opal suppose it, but neither is it a remarkable accomplishment. The world-weary sweetness of the youthful Yeats was caught unconsciously from the manner of the day—from William Morris (who was of course capable of a more vigorous mode), for example :

> Of Heaven and Hell I have no power to sing;
> I cannot ease the burden of your fears;
> Or make quick-coming death a little thing;
> Or bring again the pleasures of past years;
> Nor for my words shall ye forget your tears,
> Or hope again for aught that I can say,
> The idle singer of an empty day.

Some writers have spoken of such a tonality as if it were peculiar to end-of-the-century poetry. It, or something very like it, was, of course, the typical first phase of nineteenth-century poets generally. One would grow out of it completely and rather quickly, like Yeats or Keats, or, partially, like

Tennyson, or remain fixed in it, like Wilde and a host of
others.

The early poetry stands as one of the very last sizeable
bodies of English verse (of considerable merit) that remembers
well something of the old, old tunes, the old sweetness and
romance and simplicity and anonymity of ages that had
already passed away in England and that remained in isolated
Ireland itself only as a trace. The sense of line is already
perfectly developed in the Yeats of the mid 1890's :

> Troy passed away in one high funeral gleam.
>
> ·   ·   ·   ·   ·   ·   ·   ·   ·   ·   ·   ·   ·
>
> And at that singing he was no more wise.
>
> ·   ·   ·   ·   ·   ·   ·   ·   ·   ·   ·
>
> The quarrel of the sparrows in the eaves.

But there are only a very few poems here about which readers
have said that the tops of their heads were taken off; and in
fact few if any of the poems bear the stamp of a many-sided
and fully developed personality. The lyrical impulse normally
strong in a young man and an early fascination with the occult
(and consequently with incantatory and mnemonic qualities)
cooperated to lead Yeats to rhyme : in the one case, rhyme
functions as melody, as charm and sweetness, as a traditional
complement of English song; in the other, as an integral
feature of chant, and as a mystery or ritual, a verbal liturgy.
The Irish poet's interest in the national traditions, especially
in the heroic Celtic past, led him to simple, direct verse forms;
such interests, coupled with the youthful lyricism from which
they are after all inseparable, naturally suggested song forms—
short poems, usually in short stanzas, and often in ballad or
other quatrain forms—and also account for the abundance
of the anapest—that lilting and obvious measure—in the early
Yeats poetry. And of course the romantic inheritance prescribed euphony and "flow"—and Yeats is second to few in
obtaining them :

> He wandered by the sands of Lisadell.
>
> ·   ·   ·   ·   ·   ·   ·   ·   ·   ·   ·   ·   ·   ·   ·   ·   ·

> Were we only white birds, my beloved, buoyed out
> on the foam of the sea!
>
> . . . . , , , .
>
> "But the love-dew dims our eyes till the day
> When God shall come from the sea with a sigh
> And bid the stars drop down from the sky,
> And the moon like a pale rose wither away."

When we speak of the "later style" of Yeats we have to be careful. The later verse has its own divisions. There is a gnomic, aphoristic style in poems such as "Symbols," "Spilt Milk," "Gratitude to the Unknown Instructors," and "Old Tom Again"; a style of high-minded meditation and poignant reminiscence ("A Prayer for My Daughter," "The Wild Swans at Coole," "The Municipal Gallery Revisited," the two Coole Park poems); of pure and light lyricism ("Father and Child," "For Anne Gregory"); of earthiness and brutal frankness ("Crazy Jane and the Bishop," "Why Should Not Old Men Be Mad?"); and there is the confident, bardic—though, to my mind, seldom attractive—manner of poems like "The Gyres" and "Under Ben Bulben." It is quite a range (I have not illustrated it exhaustively) and the range itself is of course one aspect of Yeats's poetic maturity. But all these keys possess also, in contrast with the early poetry, a heightened understanding of realities and especially of the poet's own times; in its own way each key shows comprehensiveness and flexibility; there is always the richness of "a lifetime burning in every moment," and there is the fully responsible artist's sureness of touch and exorcism of vagueness, redundancy, and sentimentality. The stages of the transition from the youthful to the fully mature verse and the forces that brought such a change about have been explored by nearly everyone who has written at any length on Yeats, and in particularly felicitous detail by Thomas Parkinson in his book *W. B. Yeats: Self-Critic.*[7] To trace Yeats's progress again at this late date would be a work of supererogation. Suffice it to recall that the change begins in *The Green Helmet and Other Poems,* published in 1910, and is complete by the appearance of *The Wild Swans at Coole* in 1919, and that the achievement of a more dramatic, more colloquial, and in general surer and less nebulous style was a product of Yeats's inevitable awakening from passive aestheticism when he entered upon the writing, producing, and promoting of plays, first for the Irish Literary Theatre in 1899 and then for the Abbey in 1904. Yeats himself often acknowledged the importance of these years; in his Nobel prize speech in 1923 he made a great point of the matter. Their value can scarcely be overestimated. All that practical demand of really doing things and doing them in a certain way and having them ready at a certain time; all that confrontation with actors, dancers, musicians, and painters, and with the most real (and highly critical and even explosive) of audiences—how lucky for a young man too strongly drawn both by temperament and situation to *art pour l'art* and too much given to imagination ungrounded in a knowledge of the way of the world. Now he had to look to his language and to the foolishness or sense of his conception. He began to realize, in the first years of the twentieth century, that he had never listened acutely to contemporary speech or informal prose; and he began to see that the great body of the finest English poetry has been, without necessarily sacrificing tenderness, mystery, or transcendence, characteristically vigorous, informed with humor and irony. Poetry should be "idealized speech." Partly because Yeats worked in earnest as playwright, director, talent scout, property man, and promoter, he became a great lyric poet.

Since what we are after is not only a description of Yeats's metrical art but also an understanding of some of the relationships between the man and his metrical practice, we need to summarize his more important and more easily discernible views and inclinations, those which are so obvious from the slightest acquaintance with his life and writings as to require no documentation. For the sake of emphasis and full clarity I shall include a little of the ground covered earlier.

In his book on Yeats (*The Golden Nightingale*) in 1949 Donald A. Stauffer made an epitome of Yeats's beliefs, and the list seems to me unexceptionable, although it is far from complete. Here is Stauffer's "core": "Yeats believed in

courage, aristocracy, desire, individuality, custom and ceremony, wholeness through oppositions, and immortality".[8] In
a few cases one might want to use different terms (although
Stauffer's are sanctioned by Yeats's own usage). "Aristocracy"
might be made over into "hierarchy" or simply "order and
degree," so as to include such systems as the fascist state and
the stratified republic as well as the aristocracy proper; Yeats
believed, of course, in personal aristocracy—aristocracy of
spirit—as well. It might be well to make a few additional
qualifications. "Desire" is not to be understood in the merely
sexual sense; dynamic willing, appetite, aspiration, are included. "Immortality" is of a rather vague and not of a
Christian sort. But Yeats believed in and aspired to several
other qualities, and we have to take note of these too.

He believed in the existence of the *spiritus mundi* (or
anima mundi or Great Memory or World Soul), a repository
of significant racial memories and values, universally available, and revealed, under propitious conditions, in the form
of intuitions and symbolic images.

He believed that "the imagination has some way of light-
ing on the truth which the reason has not."[9] This notion is
of course orthodox romanticism and mysticism, though one
might add that a great many people who are not ostensibly
either mystics or romantics subscribe to it unconsciously—
sometimes, if the truth were known, consciously and hypocriti-
cally.

He stressed the irreconcilability of will and imagination,
and the desirability of a compromise, for health. Volition can-
cels out creative and contemplative power and desire; intro-
spection and composition unsuit one for action. Yeats valued
both qualities and saw that a high civilization depends on
both.

> That civilization may not sink,
> Its great battle lost,
> Quiet the dog, tether the pony
> To a distant post.

On the other hand, "Great empires are founded by lovers of

women and of money; they are destroyed by men of ideas."
Yeats knew that he could not become an athlete or explorer;
but, like Goethe, he believed in participation "for the soul's
health and the State's," and so he became moneyraiser, tower
restorer, responsible family man, school inspector, and senator,
without ceasing to be aesthete and introvert.

He hated science and utilitarianism, cultural leveling, over-
intellectualization of the personality, abstract programs for
social reform, and most of the social and aesthetic conse-
quences of industrialism. He thought materialist and rational-
ist philosophy wrong in assumptions and in values, and
spiritually debilitating. He also hated puritanic, methodistic
Irish Catholicism (he found much to admire, of course, in the
Roman church generally). Many of his contemporaries who
sought a faith went over (or were constantly on the verge of
going over) to Catholicism : Patmore, Lionel Johnson, Dowson,
Wilde. A good many drifted into or never drifted out of that
famous modern compound of doubt and indifference. A few
devised or synthesized, as did Yeats himself, odd religions of
their own : Shaw, a utopia of Supermen from Creative Evolution; Morris, a Paradise of Aesthetic Socialism; Pound, a
Benevolent Social Credit Millennium. Yeats was unique in
that the private religion he pieced together seldom strikes one
as a philosophy taking itself too seriously: one feels that Yeats
himself saw that he had sometimes arrived at metaphor rather
than final truth. Of private philosophies Yeats's is certainly
one of the least didactic or proselytizing and one having few
connections with the practical world : one could hardly
organize a movement or push a piece of legislation on the
impetus of the cones and phases of *A Vision*. There is a nice
correspondence, seldom noticed, between Yeats's persistent
aestheticism and the theoretical, unpragmatic, imaginative
nature of his elaborated world view.

Yeats preferred anything to anarchy. It is more important
to recognize this passion for order than to debate whether
Yeats was more favorable to traditional aristocracy or to the
new nationalistic and emotional order of fascism. Order within
the self and then, by extension, within the society was the

important thing; the particular type of political structure—
feudal or fascist state, limited monarchy or Burkean stratified
republic—would be almost a matter of indifference if it could
produce a settled commonwealth and at the same time encourage other Yeatsian prime values such as beauty, imaginativeness, individuality, variety, and a healthy moral tone.
There is, of course, a certain reckless and anarchic element in
Yeats's temper. He had some roots in Protestantism : he would
read the Holy Books (himself deciding which ones were holy)
and the Book of the Creatures according to his own light, and
he would represent, on the whole, the Ascendancy of Anglo-
Irish Protestantism; he liked (but would not ultimately have
chosen, either for himself or the body politic) the energy of
violence, the passion (and therefore the life) it can express—
though in point of fact he recognized (with great force and
beauty in "A Prayer for My Daughter") that violence often
expresses only a negative or perverse life. But living in the
time of Ireland's "troubles," Yeats was seldom romantic
about disorder :

> . . . the nightmare
> Rides upon sleep: a drunken soldiery
> Can leave the mother, murdered at her door,
> To crawl in her own blood, and go scot-free.
> ("Nineteen Hundred and Nineteen")

The highest good, he thought, was only "by quiet natures
understood," and the loveliest human type could only develop
"where all's accustomed, ceremonious." Yeats was immensely
dedicated to tradition, hierarchy, inherited system. There is
nothing original in this observation, but it is an important one,
and I am trying to make a fairly comprehensive résumé.

But it would hardly do to make Yeats seem quietistic; his
love of spiritual repose and outward orderliness was balanced
by a devotion to the beauty of virility. With Blake and
Lawrence he greatly admired—in a man—a strenuous and
passionate nature. It is in a man's passionate moments that he
is most fully alive; it is then that he most strongly wills his
own life and radiates it outwardly, galvanizing other men.

This heroic and passionate ideal had all sorts of ramifications. In politics, for example, it contributed to his dislike of democracy; in poetics it led him to agree with Arnold that passive suffering is not an admissible subject for poetry, and it helped produce that confident, masculine, joyous tone in his poems which fuses with his own natural modesty and quietness to produce a compelling richness one misses in most modern poets.

Yeats eventually apotheosized sexual pleasure—without, however, posing as the most virile of men himself and without advocating anything like promiscuity or other sexual experimentation. Yeats often manages the trick which few moderns have managed of being frank without being vulgar, prurient, or tediously obsessed.

He wanted to be a traditional poet, to write within the general framework of Irish and English traditions, though in his own way and out of his own experience.[10] He wanted to be thought of as an Irish bard with the attendant implications of nationalism, romance, and wisdom. In later years he was of course often skeptical or even cynical about the destiny of Ireland and the Irish, but he never relinquished his affirmation in the 1895 poem "To Ireland in the Coming Times":

> Know, that I would accounted be
> True brother of that company,
> Who sang to sweeten Ireland's wrong,
> Ballad and story, rann and song.

Yeats is thoroughly traditional too in the very bedrock of his poetics: the poet's artistry, he believed, must permeate every element of the poem, and the poem must be, finally, affirmative. Poetry is a craft: unconscious and spontaneous in its origins but a thing of skill in its final realization. To a sensitive receptor a poem's every syllable—every collocation of sounds and every segment of the semantic and rhythmic progression—registers and is adjudged as perfectly or imperfectly rendering the desired effect and as fully or less than fully consonant with the whole. Poetry postulates discipline, challenge, and order as prime values: the golden bird is in some

ways superior to ordinary birds, and in the challenge of
creating it, the artist feels a joy analogous to God's joy in
making the curlews and ravens; the reader, too, pieces the
artifact together as he reads or hears, delighting in the process and at last in his immediate intuition of the whole bird.
A poem must be well built, objectively justified. Yeats never
seriously defends any of his poems on the ground that they
represent therapy or an accurate "self-expression." A poem
must be verse, not mere effusive "warmth," "honesty," or
"urgency." "In syllabic verse, lyric, narrative, dramatic, all
syllables are important," he wrote in the now famous Introduction to the *Oxford Book of Modern Verse* (1936). Despite
his localisms and his flair for self-dramatization Yeats conceives
of poems as artifacts, not primarily as autobiographies. He
developed a strong sense of an audience, of writing not only
or mainly to unburden himself but to move someone out there.
Over the generations what has moved audiences is work that
has been intense and affirmative. Again Yeats's healthy aesthetic is much like Arnold's, and both are traditional. Even a
poem like "The Second Coming" is affirmative in that its
awesome vision implies a regret over the destruction of an
established order and therefore an affirmation of that order.
Yeats would have liked Bernard Berenson's phrase if he had
known it : works of art should be "life-enhancing."

Yeats would have agreed with Aristotle and Longinus (and
classical authority generally) that one of the principal objects
of poetry is to enthral, to create a sense of wonder. The gods
and goddesses and figures from heroic legend, the orphic
voices and inexorable historical cycles, the arcane but striking
images, of which his poetry is so full, produce color and
mystery and splendor. If we must have obscurity, let it at
least be vivid; the least poetic sort of incomprehensibility is a
dry one.

These I take to be Yeats's basic attitudes and convictions.
Finally, however, a word of warning seems necessary. One
must constantly remember that belief itself is a complex and
relatively unstable matter and that it is not, probably, fully
understood. Furthermore, the description or isolation of a

belief or attitude must always be, to some extent, a distortion of the reality itself as the individual lives it in all his unique particularities and flexibilities. And finally one must realize that, as Arland Ussher pointed out in his fine study of Yeats in *Three Great Irishmen,* Yeats's particularly protean character constantly forces one to rethink and qualify whatever statements one would make about it.

Now we need to look at the prosody of the 236 poems[11] collected between *The Wild Swans at Coole* and *Last Poems.*

(1) There is fair, though not enormous, eclecticism. Quatrains, sestets, octaves, song forms, and free lyrics (that is, short poems employing rhyme and meter but in no fixed pattern) predominate. There is a goodly sprinkling of other forms : octosyllabic and septasyllabic couplets, triplets, cinquains, sonnets, stanzas of ten or more lines, and several other unclassified forms.

(2) Yeats is as fond of sestets and octaves in the later verse as he was of quatrains in the earlier, although the quatrain (often in the form of linked or continuous quatrains) continues to be a favorite. He makes an unexpected choice of *ottava rima,* writing many of his finest poems in that stanza which had lain almost untouched by English poets since Byron.

(3) The mature Yeats almost totally avoids all meters except iambic and trochaic (or "truncated iambic"). He writes in trochaic measure rather more often than most English poets. The early poetry shows a certain fondness for anapestic meter, especially for a mixture of iambic and anapestic, as in Book I of *The Wanderings of Oisin* and "The Everlasting Voices." In the later poems Yeats calls on the anapest once in a great while, when its lightness and lilt are appropriate (as in "High Talk" or the songs from *A Full Moon in March*).

(4) There are no prosodic virtuoso pieces such as the ballade, sestina, or rondeau redoublé. There are no tour de force experiments like D. G. Rossetti's handiwork of repetend and refrain "Troy Town," or Hardy's similar essay in "The Seven Times," or Bridges's intricately feminine-rhymed "London Snow." None of Yeats's poems shows the metrical

elaborateness of pieces such as Hopkins's "Wreck of the *Deutschland*" or Dylan Thomas's "Poem in October." His only ambitiously elaborate form is the ten-line stanza that appears first, I believe, as the second part of "Meditations in Time of Civil War"; and Yeats uses it only twice more (in two sections of "Nineteen Hundred and Nineteen" and throughout "All Souls' Night"). There are no imitations of Greek, Latin, French, or other foreign verse forms.

(5) There are very few poems or sections of poems in heroic couplets (there are only three, I believe : the epigram "The Spur," the stichomythic seventh section of "Vacillation," and the third and eighth sections of the "Supernatural Songs").

(6) There is very little blank verse (of course most of the Yeats plays are in this traditional measure).

(7) There is no actual free verse, although some of the poems are metrically quite irregular.

(8) Yeats employs cadence (that is, nonmetrical or "prose rhythm" sequences) increasingly in the later verse. Cadence forms parts of lines otherwise metrical, whole lines, and in a very few cases whole poems (the cadence poems always rhyme, and so are not exactly free verse).

(9) All but a small handful of the poems rhyme.

(10) Yeats uses imperfect rhyme extensively.

(11) There is extremely little feminine rhyme. Of course most serious English poetry stays away from this type of rhyme, but Yeats stays very far indeed—much farther, for example, than Swinburne, Bridges, Hardy, or E. A. Robinson, poets roughly contemporary with Yeats and of comparable or nearly comparable range and artistry.

(12) Yeats's lines show few light endings (that is, terminations on weakly stressed syllables such as the articles and most prepositions and conjunctions) and few unrhymed feminine endings.

(13) Rarely are the lines not end-paused. There is end-pause—almost always—even when the caesura is marked by sense but not by punctuation, as in

Birth is heaped on birth
That such cannonade
May thunder time away.

The effect of end-pausing is, of course, to strengthen the sense of line and to make the close of each line emphatic. There is nothing unusual about ubiquitous end-pause, but it is more pronounced in Yeats than in many an English poet. The feature is perfectly in accord with his penchant for mnemonic and incantatory qualities.

(14) With extremely few exceptions, the terminations of Yeats's lines coincide with the termination of a clause or phrase. A new line begins a new phrase or clause.

(15) Yeats's early poetry is on the whole rather sweeter in timbre and smoother in rhythm than the poetry of his maturity, which is seldom either notably mellifluous or distinctly harsh. In short, Yeats follows the traditional practice (not always the practice of certain poets otherwise quite traditional) of shaping his medium in such a way that the poem will strike one as being phonologically neutral, which in practice means generally but not obtrusively pleasant. As usual, tradition is a good guide. Except in those rare instances when harsh effect is appropriate, verse should minimize dissonances. In verse, an unusually sensitive stream of sound, harshness seems twice as conspicuous as it would outside the poem and, unless the poet is careful to justify it, strikes the reader or listener as being as much of an objectionable idiosyncrasy there as it is in ordinary conversation.

(16) One almost never becomes conscious of alliteration and assonance in Yeats's later poetry (the devices are not notably conspicuous in the early work either). They exist, but they are used more sparingly and less obtrusively than in, say, Poe, Swinburne, or Hopkins. Yeats is modern in this respect. In modern English verse that purports to be serious, the technique of pervasive alliteration tends to create, in all but the most excellent moments of the most expert poets, a tiresome jingle; and in any case it creates aesthetic distance, carries

one further away from speech and from a tone of meditation than Yeats wanted to go.

(17) Striking instances of onomatopoeia and imitative (or "representational") rhythm are seldom encountered. Yeats's verse technique is not as unobtrusive as Wordsworth's, but it is far removed from the plangent sound-imitating or movement-imitating manner of poems like Poe's "The Bells," Byron's "Destruction of Sennacherib," or Tennyson's "Lotos-Eaters." There is nothing in Yeats as obvious as the sound-painting of a blacksmith's percussions in Hopkins's famous lines,

> When thou at the random grim forge, powerful amidst
> peers,
> Didst fettle for the great grey drayhorse his bright and
> battering sandal!

Such are the larger features of Yeats's metrical practice. If we could say how they reflect his particular character and experience, how they suit his needs and beliefs and aims, our knowledge of both the man and his poetry would be deepened, and we would even, perhaps, be able to generalize somewhat from the particular case to arrive at a subtler understanding of English poetry itself (not that I intend to undertake anything except hints in the present book). Are prosodic forms innately limited, or are all or most forms about equally suitable for all or most purposes? Do English trochaic meter and slant rhyme (to take two examples arbitrarily) lend themselves to some aims more admirably than others? Why does Yeats prefer certain meters and stanzas, and why does his preference change somewhat in his middle years? Why does he adopt a few rather unusual forms and shy away from others? Why does he persist in rhyme in an age when rhymelessness was fashion and almost dogma?

There are many questions. From Yeats himself we shall get little explicit help on them. He was a talker and a note-taker, and he talked and wrote copiously about his beliefs and biases and intuitions, about past and contemporary movements in art and society, and about poets and poetry; but he said little about versification. Comments about the sources or progress of particular poems and comments on their phrasing and imagery—this one sometimes finds in the notes and essays and letters, but rarely anything on prosody, his own or another's. Yeats stands in interesting contrast with his older contemporary Robert Bridges, who talked perhaps too much about his metrics—to the point that many people decided, mistakenly, that the Laureate's work was largely form without spirit. In Yeats's case we must rely mostly on the work itself and on what we know of the man, and proceed by cautious inference.

5

Half-Asleep or Riding upon a Journey

*I wanted to write in whatever language
comes most naturally when we soliloquise,
as I do all day long, upon the events of
our own lives or of any life where we can
see ourselves for the moment.*
—Yeats, *Autobiographies*

How DID Yeats approach the metrical aspects of composing his poems? Since he is a great poet and a striking and complex personality, his way of working is intrinsically engaging, and beyond that may provide an explanation of the fact that he wrote in an impressive variety of meters and stanzas and yet avoided many forms and greatly favored a few others.

As we have noticed, Yeats did master several, but not a great many, prosodic forms. Similarly the sheer range of his measures and stanzas, without regard to excellence of performance, is by no means narrow and yet is matched and exceeded by many English poets. His meter almost always

56

follows the standard modern practice of counting both the number of syllables and stresses within the line and distributing the stresses symmetrically (i.e., he writes what is now usually called accentual-syllabic verse). There are a few purely accentual poems ("High Talk," for example); none of the poems is purely syllabic; and there are no imitations or adaptations of classical quantitative meters. The dominant measure is the one that dominates modern English poetry : iambic Trochaic meter (our next most common) is also abundant; anapestic practically disappears after the early poetry. Length of line varies from just a few syllables to twenty or more; but as with most English poetry since the fifteenth century, tetrameters and pentameters predominate. Yeats was not a wide-ranging, experimental prosodist. He did not enter the lists with the facile metrists; he did not tease himself with the French puzzles (there is not a rondeau, villanelle, virelay, triolet, or ballade in the *Collected Poems*).[12] Familiar, ready-to-hand forms are his favorites and are at the same time, with few exceptions, his best successes : couplets, ballad and other quatrain stanzas, sestets and octaves, and irregular lyric forms —these he turns masterfully again and again.

Metrically, then, Yeats is a versatile poet, and yet not nearly so electric as, say, Bridges, Tennyson, or Swinburne. His ability to write not only competent but also fine and, in no few instances, great short poems in a variety of metrical forms reflects the intellectual and emotional scope of a poet of the first order. At the same time the very limitations of his eclecticism tell us something important about his cast of mind and help explain his reticence about the subject of prosody : he was reticent because he did not have the type of mind that very often finds in the challenge of fixed form itself a fascination and inspiration—that finds much of its subject or conception only as the predetermined form begins to suggest and dictate it. As a matter of fact, Yeats, like Jonson before him (but probably unlike most poets), often made a prose sketch of the projected poem before he set to "versing."[13] There was plenty of matter; and there was plenty of the sensible classicist in the romancing Irishman.

In his late thirties Yeats decided to try to work into his poetry some distillation of the wealth of ideas and experiences that were coming to be his amidst theater-making and frustrated but continuing courtship and Irish Catholic narrowness and civil strife. His conception of suitable poetic material widened; he began to demand that his muse bring him tougher and more intellectual fare; his love of "traditional sanctity and loveliness" would not be lost but it would be modified. However, strongly the young Yeats may have resolved not to allow his poetry to share in an intellect which he "considered impure," he could not go on suppressing opinion as it firmed and warmed into conviction : the passion which ideas so often aroused in him made expression of them in his poetry imperative. He had his convictions, and on paper he was as outspoken and courageous as the stereotype Irishman. Truly there was no dearth of substance. Some of the critics have made much of Yeats's isolation (he lived in isolated Ireland) from some of the main currents of modern change and thought. In point of fact, he knew fairly well, and in some cases very well, a great many of the important Irish and English writers of his day (Shaw, Synge, Bridges, O'Casey, Morris, Pound—the list is easier to begin than end); he also knew a host of unusually provocative, sometimes bizarre people of minor fame (Lady Gregory, Madame Blavatsky, A.E., Ernest Dowson, Lionel Johnson, Katharine Tynan, Sturge Moore, to mention some of the first names that come to mind). Yeats was not gregarious, but neither was he a recluse; dialogue and stimulation were not lacking. The occult studies provided a subject matter of their own (and Yeats did learn his magic after all, transforming disembodied spirits into solid poetic stuff, Magic into magic). The Celtic heroic past furnished the young Yeats with matter for romantic tales or episodes in verse and for melancholy brooding; later it supplied the poet with prototypes of heroic temper and cultural unity, thus inciting him to constant criticism and irony when he looked, from that perspective, at his own fragmented, leveled, mechanized, Paudeen-run world. The Irish "troubles" forced him into continual reappraisal and defense of his own political alignments and degree of commitment. The critics who take "Irish Yeats and isolated Ireland" for theme oversimplify the facts; not their least mistake is to forget that it is better for a poet to know the whole inside and out of a local but typical struggle than to be "informed" in the good modern sciolistic way about current international events and the "course of modern history." The local is often the universal writ small and therefore vividly. Eclectic sophistication seldom makes poetry, and poetry of color and force never. The situation in Ireland in the first decades of the twentieth century was almost as propitious for Yeats as was that in Elizabethan England which enabled Shakespeare to realize his powers.

Critics have also made much of the fact that Yeats was a "literary" writer, an aesthete. The point is well taken, but of course the concept is relative : if Arthur Symons is an aesthete, then Yeats is a stern lawgiver; if Dobson and Swinburne are literary, Yeats is unlettered. There is no trace in him of the barrenness, triviality, miniaturism, and excessive interest in verbal or stanzaic form that afflict the merely or preponderantly literary. There is a manliness and roundness in Yeats, and his choosing "perfection of the art" over life and not obscure it. The metrics of the poetry by which (on the whole) he has been and will continue to be judged—that which he wrote from about 1910 onward—is a direct reflection of this combination of balanced temper and basically quite fortunate circumstance. Characteristically bringing to the act of composition burning insight and conviction and too much, rather than too little, to say, Yeats tended to seize upon the more common, the more likely measures and stanzas. Vision and urgency will send more of our poets to iambs than to amphibrachs and alcaics. The iambic tune is familiar, and modern English diction and syntax themselves seem to recommend it for serious verse (an iambic measure, accentual or quantitative, is in fact ubiquitous in Germanic and Romance tongues generally). Similarly one can tell a couplet or quatrain what to do, but with a ballade or chant royal one's progress must depend heavily on the heuristic suggestions of an intricate form which, checking at every turn the natural phrase and the logical sequence, establishes great aesthetic distance. Hence Yeats's habitual quatrains, tetrameter couplets, stanzas of six and eight lines, and free lyrics.[14] Quatrains, sestets, and octaves alone make up two thirds of his poems, the latter two forms (of which there are several variants, of course) appearing abundantly in the poems of his maturity—natural developments from his early favorite, the quatrain, and no doubt called for to provide greater working room for the richer, more experienced man of middle and old age.

At the same time there is a counter principle. Since Yeats was a prolific poet, and since he did not, as some poets have done, censor out all tones and subjects save a very few, it was inevitable that he would write in a variety of forms. In the round, then, it was a case of abundant, varied thought and feeling sponsoring the varied forms necessary to carry them, and of form being made to follow the contours of meditation —"soliloquy"—and of ordinary prose syntax and speech locutions, and not so much a case of arbitrarily selected pre-existing form inviting and demanding feeling and idea to fill it. This way is not the only way of poetic genius, but it was Yeats's typical approach. The moderately limited number of his forms, their relative simplicity, and the large number of irregular forms suggest (as does all other evidence) that he did not often take his inspiration from metrical form itself, as Dobson, Swinburne, and Bridges often undoubtedly did. His forms suggest an overriding absorption in thought, passion, and icon, and a relative indifference to cadenzas of metrical artistry. He had, according to his biographer Hone[15] and others, no true ear for music (and in fact, as is well known, little patience with it); and he was no linguist. Hone remarks in the *Biography* that Yeats "read books on prosody, but could never remember what was in them,"[16] and goes on to quote a revealing remark the aged poet made in a letter to Edith Shackleton : "You will notice how bothered I am when I get to prosody, because it is the most certain of my instincts, but the subject of which I am most ignorant."[17] And in a letter to Dorothy Wellesley in 1935, in a tone slightly self-reproachful, Yeats confesses that "poetry is all instinct with me."[18] In the *Biography* Hone says that Yeats's ear for the sound of speech was so sensitive "that it outran comprehension,"[19] a judgment sometimes questioned, but confirmed by most of the people who came to know Yeats well or hear him read or criticize readings or play rehearsals (curiously, though, he could not, despite this gift, write peasant dialect reliably, and consulted Lady Gregory when he needed it).

Yeats, then, did not, as some good poets have done, make a practice of lovingly—but more or less arbitrarily—studying now one verse form and now another, allowing the form so to implant its pattern in the mind that eventually (and with some luck) it "invites the words into their places" (to use a fine phrase of Robert Bridges), bringing to the poet not infrequently much of the very substance, the very ideas, images, words, of the poem. Yeats early got his tune—set his habits of composition to a few relatively simple and speechlike and songlike forms and techniques and, except for an occasional innovation, rested content in them. The modes and patterns became second nature to him, so that in his maturity he was neither like the one poet who delights in extempore metrical acrobatics, nor like the other, who goes to new forms as to an outwardly dry oasis which after much digging ultimately yields some precious water. Yeats's choices in prosody show us, I believe, that he has so much to say and is so intent on saying it without undue delay—his magnificent artistic sense and conscience would of course greatly delay him—that he repeatedly takes up the forms in which he has acquired the most practice and which are at the same time among the easier and more traditional forms for an English poet. He had relatively little need and no great inclination to search out new forms, to see what good thing the technical challenge of a villanelle or sestina would yield. I repeat that one can hardly avoid a conclusion that there are good poets who find the heuristic value of diverse and relatively complicated forms remarkably congenial and valuable. In such cases the challenge of the form brings the poet conceptions and images in which his mind is not naturally rich (I am not, of course, proposing that metrically experimental poets are necessarily poor in conception and imagery: Donne, Browning, and Auden are poets as fertile conceptually and imagistically as prosodically). This sort of poet is well gifted with verbal sensitivity and sometimes with formal structural ability as well, but he does not have the image-laden mind of a Keats or the narrative fertility of a Chaucer or Spenser or the memoir-making and self-analyzing and self-dramatizing impulse of a Yeats. Austin Dobson, Swinburne, Poe, and Sidney Lanier are such poets; one of our finest artists of this stamp (and a poet admired by Yeats though not generally by Yeatsians) is Robert Bridges. But Yeats is of another cut. His thought is not completely systematic, like that of a professional philosopher, and often it may seem perverse or bizarre; but it is there; there is plenty of insight and observation and synthesis. Yeats led for many years a crowded, ambitious, dramatic, at times adventurous life. From his earliest years he moved in a varied crowd, which was also a crowd that sparkled with various excellences and sometimes burned with greatness. His times were not dull. And his mind happened to be such that he worked from a rich store of reveries and reminiscences. It was all very fortunate: in quieter and less demanding circumstances Yeats's innate aestheticism might have triumphed utterly, and he would have become only one of the better minor poets of his time. But in all that solidity of his there was no need or place for filigree, academic exercise, casual experiment, or mere virtuosity—little call of any sort to go beyond the forms ready-to-hand.

Still it would be quite misleading to say that Yeats wrote "spontaneously," that his lines usually came as fast as he could get them down, and that nothing then remained but to lop off the excess here, add a link there, and alter a word here and there. Except for very short stretches, probably no poet— except the fictitious poet of the popular imagination—has ever written poetry of a high order that way. Even the rather prosaic Matthew Arnold complained that he had to tear himself to pieces to write a poem. Shakespeare's facility is probably exaggerated, and Southey's produced a body of poetry the world has willingly let die. In any event, Yeats sought the discipline (and joy) of working to a form, and composition was by his own admission almost always painfully slow. That he made such poor time despite his having made the old verse tunes second nature and despite his having frequently made beforehand a prose sketch is testimony to a noble conception of artistry. He was able to be prolific only because he worked so relentlessly. It was even true that occasionally Yeats wrote out the rhyme scheme of a stanza and then proceeded to try to find content to go with the scheme and the particular rhyme words tentatively chosen. The manuscripts show us that he sometimes worked that way, depending to some degree on the heuristic pull of the scheme to produce a coherent poetic sequence. But of course rhyme is so difficult to manage in a rhyme-poor language like ours, and it is so sensitive a linguistic detail, that every poet who sets out to write serious rhyming verse must work in this manner to some extent, laying out the mold clearly before him and then listening to the perhaps manifold suggestions whispered by the structure and by the tentatively selected rhyme words; the poet gets his bearings and begins his true course partly from these intimations and possibilities. When an English poet—especially a modern one, who not only inherits a dearth of rhyme but who no longer possesses the Elizabethan syntactical liberties that helped compensate for that paucity—decides to try his hand at an elaborate or repetitively rhymed stanza, he needs all the help he can get. It is only in such complex schemes that we find Yeats thus maneuvering in his worksheets. In his case the laid-out pattern was more a convenience to facilitate the crystallization of an already saturated conception than a heuristic structure designed to suggest conception itself. It was not like playing *bouts rimés,* in which one begins with an empty head and a handful of arbitrary words that, brooded upon, will (hopefully) produce a passable poem. In many instances Yeats's jotted-down words were no doubt called up out of some already clarified theme and iconography. "Here are some of the words I am going to need in places of prominence if I do anything with this theme," he says, and sets them down. We can be certain that he sometimes did exactly that. To take a single instance : early in the composition of the second part of his "Vacillation" he made a list of seven rhyme words : "bough," "leaf," "dew," "chief," "anew," "belief," "grief." The stanza that ultimately developed envisions a tree, a symbolically complex tree. Yeats's whole creative process in beginning and working out this stanza was governed by the image and conception of the tree. Now notice the rhyme words : five are nouns, the first three concrete and the final two abstract. The concrete nouns come right out of the image : they occur first in the set, and they are all descriptive of a tree. And as matters worked out, these are the only three rhyme words Yeats retained in the final version of this section of the poem. His mind was dominated by images charged with symbolic potential; the rhyme and stanza layouts one very occasionally finds in his worksheets existed primarily to aid in getting substance to gel, not to supply basic substance itself. Before 1910 Yeats had already staked everything on the fortune of an interesting, rather than uneventful, life: "I shall, if good luck or bad luck make my life interesting, be a great poet," he says in the autobiographies,[20] and he goes on to say that he wanted "metrical forms that seemed old enough to have been sung by men half-asleep or riding upon a journey."[21] His life turned out to be interesting, and his love of the past was not one of his "masks." He did not need to enter the labyrinth of an intricate form to find his excitement : his head was already full of dragons.

Intellectual and emotional range produced a variety of metrical forms; conviction and a general fertility, pressing for expression and conjoined with a love of the traditional, reduced the potential variety to the more familiar and accessible forms; a desire to create a mnemonic, incantatory effect and at the same time to stay fairly close to speech, to the impulse and spontaneity of the moment, made him keep up his rhyme and meter yet permit a lifelike irregularity in much of the meter and some angularity in the rhyme. That, I believe, is the essential rationale of Yeats's unity in variety.

6

A Measure for Speech

*. . . All over-rhythmical writing is at once felt to
be affected and finical and wholly lacking in passion,
owing to the monotony of its superficial polish.*

—Longinus

*. . . The iambic is, of all measures, the most
colloquial: we see it in the fact that conversational
speech runs into iambic lines more frequently than
into any other kind of verse.*

—Aristotle

DESPITE the metrical irregularity of a good many of Yeats's later poems, few of them get altogether away from meter, and the meter, whether in the less regular or more regular poems, is almost invariably iambic or trochaic. Yeats almost ignores the existence of the dactyl, and rarely uses anapests (outside the early verse) except as occasional substitutions in iambic lines. Iambic and trochaic are, of course, easily our commonest measures. Trisyllabic meters, owing to their speed and their tendency to be overrhythmical,[22] have proved useful in the main only for special purposes, as for lilt and comedy (Yeats's hearty "High Talk" is full of them). Possibly our present vocabulary and syntax are hostile to the formation of unstrained sequences of them; and the fact that they are rare— relative to iambs and trochees—in speech and prose makes them seem rather literary and exotic. Perhaps it is the tendency of modern poetry toward a realistic and pedestrian vein, as much as any intrinsic linguistic difficulty, that accounts for the near-disappearance of trisyllabic verse in serious work. In any case, Yeats's devotion to iambic meter is further evidence that he was not a poet who took a strong intellectual interest in prosodic form in the abstract or who greatly needed to study new or unusual verse forms for the inspiration they might bring him. It was perfectly natural for him to stick, for the most part, with the meter most ready to hand.

But before I go further, it may be desirable to establish the fact that Yeats is, in truth, an iambic poet. Such a demonstration would be unnecessary (or would have seemed unnecessary to me), were it not for Thomas Parkinson's misgivings in his study *W. B. Yeats: The Later Poetry* (Berkeley, 1964). Parkinson is an able scholar who writes clearly and knows prosody. His position is not a dogmatic one, but he frankly doubts the relevance of the old "foot" system to an interpretation of Yeats's verse. He is inclined to believe that Yeats measured his decasyllables, not by the system of iambic feet, but by the simpler system of syllable count. In this view Yeats is, in short, very often a poet whose prosody is syllabic (like French poetry). Parkinson's defense of this minority view (nearly everyone has already assumed that Yeats was as iambic a poet as Wordsworth or Shakespeare) rests, if I understand it, mainly on two points. First, the poems of Yeats that we would normally call pentameter or iambic pentameter are more regular in their observance of the rule of ten syllables to a line than in their "iambic" quality; many apparent infractions of decasyllabism are to be explained on the basis of elision (with this later point no one, I believe, need have any quarrel). Secondly, Parkinson found no "foot" notations in any of the

Yeats worksheets he examined. I am unable to determine whether Parkinson would really deny the existence, in the bulk of Yeats's poetry, of an iambic measure or "duple rising rhythm," or whatever one cares to call a general pattern of weak stress followed by strong stress; he simply emphasizes Yeats's decasyllabism and is skeptical about the applicability of the unit or foot system.

The weight of tradition is the best answer to Parkinson's view. To my knowledge, readers have all but unanimously perceived the iambic—let us not quibble over mere terms—rhythm of the memorable Yeats lines and poems. Yeats's iambic pentameters are often loose, but so are those of many other poets. Nor does Yeats, in point of fact, observe decasyllabism with unusual meticulousness. In the blank verse of the plays and in the rhyming and unrhyming pentameters of the poems alike there is wide variation in the syllable count, and by no means all of these variations are to be accounted for by elision. "The Municipal Gallery Revisited" is not untypical of the pentameter of Yeats's verse from 1910 on, and in that poem variation from the ten-syllable norm almost becomes the rule. In the first stanza of that octave poem, for example, lines three and four are Alexandrines :

> Casement upon trial, half hidden by the bars,
> 1   2 3 4   5 6   7   8   9 10 11   12
>
> Guarded; Griffith staring in hysterical pride,
>   1 2   3   4   5 6 7   8   91011   12

and line eight is a thirteener (Yeats would read "revolution'ry") :

> A revolutionary soldier kneeling to be blessed.
> 1   23 4 5 6   7   8   9   10 11 12   13

The second stanza continues with similar disregard for any rigidly decasyllabic standard :

> An Abbot or Archbishop with an upraised hand
> 1   2   3 4   5   6 7   8 9 10   11   12
>
> Blessing the Tricolour. "This is not," I say,
>   1 2   3   4 5 6   7 8   9 10 11

"The dead Ireland of my youth, but an Ireland
1 2   3   4 5 6   7 8 9 10   11
The poets have imagined, terrible and gay."
1 2 3   4   5 6   7   8 9 10 11   12

Nor is the lack of foot notations in Yeats's worksheets convincing evidence for the poet's having little or no truck with the foot system. Many poets' worksheets—most, I would guess—lack such notations. And there is the fact that the word "foot" does sometimes appear in Yeats's few comments on prosody. His remarks on the opening line of *Paradise Lost* in "A General Introduction for My Work" are clearly couched in terms of the old foot prosody so familiar to us all. He scans the famous line, speaks of its "five feet," and even borrows Robert Bridges's term "contrapuntal" to indicate the character of a rhythm in which the natural phrasings of " passionate speech" play against the theoretical metric norm :

> The contrapuntal structure of the verse, to employ a term adopted by Robert Bridges, combines the past and present. If I repeat the first line of *Paradise Lost* so as to emphasize its five feet I am among the folk singers—"Of mán's first disobédience and the fruit," but speak it as I should I cross it with another emphasis, that of passionate prose—"Of mán's fírst disobédience and the frúit," or "Of mán's fírst dísobedience and the frúit"; the folk song is still there, but a ghostly voice, as unvariable possibility, an unconscious norm.[23]

Parkinson himself noticed (p. 199) Yeats's use of the word "feet" in a MS notation on Cowley's poem on solitude. Cowley was one of Yeats's favorites among the Metaphysicals. The poem on solitude no doubt recommended itself to Yeats by its feeling not only for quietness but for trees, one of the few natural images that moved Yeats deeply. Here is Cowley's first stanza :

> Hail, old *Patrician* Trees, so great and good!
> Hail ye *Plebeian* under wood!
> Where the Poetique Birds rejoyce,
> And for their quiet Nests and plentious Food,
> Pay with their grateful voice.

Yeats's notation is as follows:

    5 feet good
    4   „ wood
    4   „ rejoice
    5   „ food
    3   „ voice

"The Mother of God" is the poem Yeats modeled on Cowley's
pattern. I quote the first stanza :

> The threefold terror of love; a fallen flare
> Through the hollow of an ear;
> Wings beating about the room;
> The terror of all terrors that I bore
> The Heavens in my womb.

Parkinson, apparently unable to find the unit or foot system
in Yeats's poem but perceiving that Yeats's lines follow Cowley's in stress count, says that Yeats must have meant "stresses"
when he wrote "feet." But the poem does, in fact, follow
Cowley's pattern, and Yeats meant "feet" when he wrote
"feet." In his finished poem Yeats deviated from the Cowley
model by truncating lines two and three in the first two
stanzas. The third stanza follows Cowley's meter exactly. It is
the usual story : Yeats's art of verse looks to tradition and to
models, and at the same time it innovates.

Still, the matter is a bit complicated. I do not say that
Yeats worked to the foot system as Campion or Bridges sometimes worked to it. That is not the only alternative to sylla-
bism. With Parkinson I feel almost certain that when Yeats
was composing or revising, he did not look to his rhythms in
terms of distinct little metrical units ("I must change this to a
trochee . . . here is a fine spot for an anapestic substitution . . ."). What Yeats did, undoubtedly, was what most other
English poets have done. He knew and loved the traditional
modern meter (that is, accentual-syllabic—and iambic). He
may not have thought of it in terms of "feet"; he heard the
rising rhythm and acquired the sense of line. The whole process was a matter of learning and adopting an old familiar

tune, a pattern of alternating unstressed and stressed syllables running to about the length of a normal breath, and then, usually after a pause, starting again. In any event, the iambic rhythm is there for everyone to hear :

And that|enquir|ing man|John Synge|comes next,

That dy|ing chose|the liv|ing world|for text

. . . .

And may|her bride|groom bring|her to|a house

where all's|accus|tomed, cer|emon|ious

. . . .

An ag|ed man|is but|a pal|try thing

. . . .

Of what|is past,|or pass|ing, or|to come

. . . .

I pace|upon the bat|tlements|and stare

. . . .

Many|ingen|ious love|ly things|are gone

. . . .

A six|ty-year-|old smil|ing pub|lic man

. . . .

I sought|a theme|and sought|for it|in vain

Throughout this book I have adopted both the terminology and methodology of the classical or quantitative or foot system of scansion. In so doing—let me repeat—I do not wish to imply that Yeats necessarily or habitually thought about metrical structure in terms of feet or in terms of the rest of the classical apparatus—elisions, substitutions, etc. At least, it is difficult to believe that he encumbered himself with a rigid unit system the way Horace and Vergil presumably did. That he played by ear, and that many or most of our poets have also done so, I would be the last to doubt. But he did use the old iambic measure anyway, and the whole range of the classical or traditional structure—the elisions, the substitutions, the catalectic and hypercatalectic endings—is there. The engagement of imaginative writing is not exactly like laying bricks; it is a process of empathy and intuition, not of willful mechanics (yet one is, after all—if one is working in verse—writing to a theoretical metrical pattern). Even a prosodist-poet (Dobson, Bridges, Lanier), in the heat and anguish of writing, usually has to feel his developing music too intensely (to say nothing of his necessary concentration on image, diction, connection) to give much overt thought to the notes. The classical apparatus, as we have adopted it, seldom pretends to be anything more than a convenience in allowing us to determine the metrical structure of the line. I have employed it here because it is the most familiar and, as I think, still the most useful approach to scansion wherever English verse sets up as its pattern a control of the number of syllables and number and positions of stresses within the line. Yeats himself would have welcomed here, as he was ready to welcome almost everywhere, the spirit of tradition. Readers looking for a more detailed defense of the traditional scansion might consult the treatment of the subject offered in Joseph B. Mayor's *Chapters on English Metre* (London, 1901) or in the book co-authored by the present writer and Karl Shapiro, *A Prosody Handbook* (New York, 1965).

I have already suggested some important reasons for Yeats's adherence to iambic meter. There are certainly others.

Once we are out of the early period, we find that the short poems characteristically have a dramatic quality. They are often high-pitched, incantatory, often personal in a proud, intense, assertive way. Frequently Yeats is trying to achieve rhythms that suggest a speaking voice—now declamation, now the low key of a tired old man or of Crazy Jane—rather than the refined, artful movement of Bridges's lyrics or the lovely, marmoreal rhythms of the *Faerie Queene* or *The Eve of St. Agnes* or many of his own early poems. And of course iambic is (as both English poetry and drama have long since demon-strated) the most feasible meter for dialogue. To make a point, one might say that Yeats was dignified and meditative about half the time and indignant or passionate the other half; and English anapests and dactyls have not proved to be a viable idiom for either the former qualities or the latter. We have to remember that in his maturity Yeats was working toward an idiom that would allow him packed thought and observation; and there is not, in English, any significant body of metered thought and observation that is not also iambic. Further, it is certain that iambic is the only measure that could have allowed Yeats the great metrical liberties he pursued in his later years—pursued partly, no doubt, because of the increase in realism often attendant upon ripe years and partly because of his increasing (and not necessarily wise) attraction to the earthy and the irrational. Poets who live to maturity or old age often, perhaps normally, move—if they change at all—from a tighter to a looser metrics : Shakespeare, Milton, Blake, Byron, Bridges, Rilke, Yeats—certainly one could think of many names. The young poet loves romance and statuary, the mature or old poet the illusion of artlessness and conversation.

By his fourth book of poems, *In the Seven Woods* (1904), Yeats shows complete and continual mastery of an iambic pentameter suitable for the short poem (he had of course perfected dramatic blank verse as early as *The Countess Cathleen,* 1892). Here and there in the early books there are, of course, faultless sequences of pentameters—I refer to the integration of meter and rhetoric; these (or, indeed, any) lines from "The Man Who Dreamed of Faeryland," for example:

> Were not the worms that spired about his bones
> A-telling with their low and reedy cry,
> Of how God leans His hands out of the sky,
> To bless that isle with honey in His tones;
> That none may feel the power of squall and wave. . . .
> (*Poems,* Boston: 1895)

The sense of line is fully developed; the movement is flexible; monotony is avoided; rhetorical emphases are distributed clearly. But few of the earlier pentameter poems will compare with the best in the 1904 book. In "The Folly of Being Comforted" and "Adam's Curse" there are not only memorable single lines, such as,

> The fire that stirs about her, when she stirs,

but tightly coherent and musical yet conversational sequences:

> I had a thought for no one's but your ears:
> That you were beautiful, and that I strove
> To love you in the old high way of love;
> That it had all seemed happy, and yet we'd grown
> As weary-hearted as that hollow moon.

In the next book (*The Green Helmet and Other Poems*, 1910) the pentameter poems are the best ones: "No Second Troy," "Reconciliation," "The Fascination of What's Difficult," "Upon a House Shaken by the Land Agitation" have worn well.

The meter itself, whether in these or in much later pentameter poems, is handled in pretty much a traditional way. Yeats's pentameter never becomes as loose as, say, that which one often finds in the plays of John Webster. When he wants to write in the freest rhythms, he almost always uses lines shorter or longer than pentameter, or else he abandons the iambic norm altogether. For the Yeats pentameter traditional modes of variation are the rule: the use of synalephic elision:

> Around|me the images|of thir|ty years

or the inclusion of a single, light extrametrical syllable, a device that is best seen, to my thinking, as a form of elision, though it may also be interpreted as introducing an anapestic foot:

> The in|tellec|tual sweet|ness of|those lines

> The in|tellec|tual sweet|ness of|those lines

the substitution of a trochaic for an iambic foot (inversion):

Sound of|a stick upon the floor, a sound

the substitution of one ionic foot (.. //) for two iambs :

But the dark changed|to red, and torches shone.

As in Milton and Shakespeare (and most other poets, for that matter), the final foot of a pentameter line is seldom anything but iambic. When a line is allowed an extra syllable in its midst (rather than at the end) Yeats almost invariably follows the classic practice of assigning this extrametrical syllable an inferior accent or following it with a vowel or semi-vowel into which it glides, so that it may be elided and thus not really break the metrical pattern. The traditional practice is a sound one : the effect of surprise produced by a break in the meter should not be a violent one (unless, of course, the break is designed to heighten the representation of some violence in the subject). But perhaps it will be well to pause here for a moment, since the theory of elided syllables in English verse is not universally understood and has been, in fact, terribly obfuscated by the haste or confusion of many commentators.

An elided syllable is not meant to be unduly slurred; at least, marked slurring has not been the reading practice of our poets (English has long been developing, of course, an unfortunate tendency to slur almost everything). And certainly the elided or fused syllable is not often meant to be dropped altogether. For example, we are to enunciate both the *ly* and the *I* in Donne's line

Yet dear|ly I love|you, and|would be|loved fain,

and we are not asked to reduce "miraculous" to a trisyllable in

And a|mirac|ulous strange|bird shrieks|at us.

An elided syllable is simply an unstressed extra syllable introduced into a line in order to provide welcome relief from the regular pattern or to bring into the line a slight suggestion of the ease of ordinary speech or prose. Since by long habituation the English ear tends to associate physical stress with semantic importance, and since the variation created by extra-metrical elided syllables is designed to provide only relief and richness, the syllable dare not be a very prominent one; if it is too prominent, it will tend to alert the mind to look for something semantically prominent at that point. An elision may be said to break the meter without breaking it: it breaks the pattern only slightly in fact and not at all in theory.

Yeats favors three ways of working in the extra syllable. He elides (1) two abutting vowels or semi-vowels:

> The ceremony of innocence is drowned

(2) the weakest syllable of a polysyllable:

> May she|become|a flour|ishing hid|den tree,

. . . .

> Consid|ering that,|all hat|red driv|en hence,

. . . .

> A beau|tiful seat|ed boy;| a sac|red bow

(3) a monosyllable that is an auxiliary or otherwise static verb form and that consequently receives but scant attention from the mind or breath. This latter construction occurs constantly in all of Yeats's iambic verse. Here, for example, are the opening lines of "Her Praises":

> 1 She is foremost of those that I would hear praised.
> 2 I have gone about the house, gone up and down
> 3 As a man does who has published a new book,
> 4 Or a young girl dressed out in her new gown,
> 5 And though I have turned the talk by hook or crook
> 6 Until her praise should be the uppermost theme,
> 7 A woman spoke of some new tale she had read,
> 8 A man confusedly in a half dream
> 9 As though some other name ran in his head.

Only three lines (4, 8, 9) are syllabically normal. Each of the other six has eleven syllables instead of ten, and in each case but one (6) the extra syllable is a "would," "have," "has," or "had," that is, a weak, auxiliary verb form habitually slighted in English articulation. This construction—it is not original with Yeats, but he is unusually fond of it—gives rise to an interesting and peculiarly felicitous effect as of counterpoint; we are unconsciously tempted to read the lines as if they made the subject-verb contraction :

> I've gone about the house, gone up and down
> As a man does who's published a new book . . .
> . . . .
> And though I've turned the talk by hook or crook. . . .

The beauty of the construction lies in the fact that the effect of contraction is actually suggested to the mind and tongue, though actual contraction would have made the homely but still elevated and romantic tone of this poem impossible and the lines too regular metrically. The same practice is found in the blank verse of the plays. If ever a poet had his form and broke it too, here is an instance.

Yeats's favorite spot for trochaic substitution (that is, inversion of the iambic foot) is, as is the case with most English poets, the initial foot of the line:

> Únder|this cradle-hood and coverlid . . .
>
> Béauty|to make a stranger's eyes distraught . . .
>
> Hélen|being chosen found life flat and dull . . .
>
> Héarts are|not had as a gift but hearts are earned . . .
>
> Prósper|but little has dried up of late.

Occasionally he allows the trochee farther along in the line:

> Nor knew,|drúnken|with sing|ing as|with wine,
>
> Nor beau|ty bórn|out of|its own|despair

though (as in English poetry generally) the final foot is almost never trochaic (the effect of a trochee in the final foot is, of course, to feminize and thus drastically alter the character of the line).

Before we leave the subject of Yeats's chief measure, we should remark one other feature : his partiality in his blank verse (whether poem or play) to the anapestic substitution. Such substitutions in his rhymed iambic verse are far less frequent (perhaps—after years of thought I can offer nothing more than a guess here—because the effects of speed and freedom they introduce are more consonant with the "realism" of dialogue than with the usually tighter, more dignified, and more hieratic mode of rhymed verse). Here are two sets of lines (the first from *Deirdre*, an early play, the second from "Ego Dominus Tuus") to illustrate the blank verse anapests:

> We have|no coun|try but|the roads|of the world.
>
> Then you|should know|that all|things change|in the world.
>
> He found|the un|persuad|able jus|tice, he found
>
> The most|exalt|ed la|dy loved|by a man.

Again, Yeats is metrically orthodox : the anapestic substitution is not an uncommon habit of blank verse (though Shakespeare and Milton generally disallow the practice). Being traditional and natural—natural because both the anapest and the iamb are rising measures—Yeats's usage perhaps requires no explanation. And yet one is tempted (not by the charm of speculation but by the impact of the blank verse) to suggest a further reason why the graceful and undulant anapest found favor in the blank verse : it is the most lyrical of possible substitutions. The lyrical impulse is, after all, dominant in Yeats, and his blank-verse plays are lyrics for the stage.

Outside the plays, of course, Yeats uses blank verse sparingly; only five poems, I believe, are cast in it after 1919, and most of these are dialogue poems. Like most poets writing in English, Yeats felt that rhyme adds strength and color to lyrical verse, adds music and mnemonic power and greater architectural clarity and unity. His own bent is strongly for the ritualistic, incantatory, suggestive, and simply pleasurable effects of rhyme. And the many plays gave him a diet rich enough in blank verse.

7

A Bolder Measure

*. . . The iambic and the trochaic tetrameter are stirring
measures, the latter being akin to dancing.*

—Aristotle

"Words alone are certain good."

ALTHOUGH this memorable line occurs in the earliest poem
Yeats saved for the *Collected Poems*, there is nothing in the
early verse to indicate that he would someday write a great
body of trochaic poetry. But he stands, in fact, as one of the
great masters of that falling measure.[24] He takes up the challenge of its dangerous intensity and joins the company of
Shakespeare, Blake, and Coleridge. Perhaps few or none of
his trochaics quite match the Shakespeare trochaic songs or
"The Tyger" or certain parts of *The Rime of the Ancient
Mariner*; but he is often only just below such touchstones.
The quantity too is impressive; Yeats uses the meter more
often than most (perhaps more often than any) English poets
whose work is of comparable quality.

Trochaic tetrameter is the favorite form, as it is with
English poets generally. "Swift's Epitaph" is in this measure:

Swift has|sailed in|to his|rest;
Savage indignation there
Cannot lacerate his breast . . .

and so is "Under Ben Bulben" :

> Swear by what the sages spoke
> Round the Mareotic Lake
> That the Witch of Atlas knew,
> Spoke and set the cocks a-crow . . .
>
> Irish poets, learn your trade,
> Sing whatever is well made,
> Scorn the sort now growing up . . .

and the brief fourth section of "Nineteen Hundred and Nineteen" :

> We, who seven years ago
> Talked of honour and of truth,
> Shriek with pleasure if we know
> The weasel's twist, the weasel's tooth.

Many of the iambic tetrameter poems are heavily laden with trochaic lines. "Why Should Not Old Men be Mad?" opens with a trochaic couplet :

> Why should not old men be mad?
> Some have known a likely lad . . .

"Lapis Lazuli," "The Three Hermits," "The Realists," "Mohini Chatterjee," "The Old Man and the Echo," part three of "The Tower"—these and several other of the short poems are dominantly or partly trochaic. A number of the poems in *Words for Music Perhaps* are in this meter or are built of a medley of iambic and trochaic meters together with lines of cadence. The opening poem of this latter group, "Crazy Jane and the Bishop," shows such a mixture :

Bring me the blasted oak	(*trochaic*)
That I, midnight upon the stroke,	(*iambic*)
(*All find safety in the tomb.*)	(*trochaic*)
May call down curses on his head	(*iambic*)

> Because of my dear Jack that's dead, (*iambic*)
> Coxcomb was the least he said: (*trochaic*)
> *The solid man and the coxcomb* . . . (*nonmetrical*)

A rhyming, basically octosyllabic poem that moves continually back and forth between iambic and trochaic meter becomes one of the characteristic forms of Yeats's later verse. It is also, of course, a traditional English form; in fact, probably only quatrains and iambic pentameters have been more favored, at least until quite recent times. The form is a flexible one: irregularly alternating iambic and trochaic tetrameters have welcomed poetry as disparate as Blake's songs and epigrams and Coleridge's narratives.

Obviously Yeats found in trochaic meter certain qualities that suited some of his tastes and aims. The adaptability and the tradition-blessed aura of iambic-trochaic verse I have already noted. Another thing Yeats pursued almost from the beginning, though more urgently as he grew older, was metrical forms in which the freedom and something of the lively or stately cadences of ordinary and of declamatory speech could play some part. Since a poem that alternates iambic and trochaic lines is not as smooth as a straight sequence of either meter, and since an irregular alternation is more ragged and colloquial still, I think we should view Yeats's partiality to this form as evidence of his increasing interest in cadence as it could be incorporated into a form that would yet remain richer in prosodic structure and generally more musical or sonorous than the free verse then being written by so many of his English and American contemporaries. Also, an iambic-trochaic or iambic-trochaic-cadence medley is one that imposes few restrictions on the poet in the heat of composition. The distance between the poet's developing thought and the rendering of the thought is diminshed. This is only to say that as verse forms go, this one is simple and "natural." As such it is no surprise to encounter it in a poet of Yeats's stamp.

English trochaic measure has never threatened, and unless extraordinarily radical linguistic changes occur, probably never will threaten, the dominance of the iamb. Time has run on, and the trochee has proved most useful as a measure for the short span or as a spice in iambic meat. No doubt there is some element of chance in its failure to make a stronger bid, but there are probably fundamental linguistic deterrents as well. It may be, as many prosodists and grammarians have argued, that both our vocabulary and syntax favor the iambic at the expense of other meters. No doubt there are other difficulties, too. A trochaic line is infinitely difficult to vary internally. The most viable substitute foot is the dactyl, but dactyls tend to create a rhythm equally as formal and exotic as pure trochaic. Further, trochaic meter tends to make the first word of every line enormously emphatic; yet it is a rare poem whose thought and feeling can justify such recurring initial emphasis.

Trochaic, then, is a meter that strikes us as being emphatic and extraordinary. It seems even more aesthetically distant than the anapestic rhythm : the latter is rather like iambic meter with extra syllables in the rising. Consequently a trochaic measure seems most appropriate when the "subject" of the poem has something unusual about it—if only unusual intensity. It is well adapted to the macabre or to the gnomic incantation or, at the other end of the spectrum, to light things and endearing nonsense (the aesthetic distance created by the formal and emphatic meter seems happily incongruous with the familiar or lively subject or mood; bagatelles, non-sense verse, high merriment—seldom is this kind of poetry iambic). The trochee, it would seem, must always chant or dance or jig. Mother Goose is often trochaic (and dactylic and anapestic):

> Goosey,|goosey|gander . . .
>
> Jack, be|nimble,|Jack, be|quick . . .
>
> Polly,|put the|kettle|on . . .

The emphatic tone of imperative verse lends itself to trochaics :

> Foot it featly here and there . . .
> Swing your partner round and round . . .

The emphatic nature of the meter accommodates it to the emphatic manner of primitive or "naïve" rhythmical utterance :

> Little lamb, who made thee?
> Dost thou know who made thee . . .

When the context is intense and aphoristic, the wisdom can be chanted into us mnemonically :

> A Robin Redbreast in a Cage
> Puts all Heaven in a Rage . . .
> The wild deer, wandering here & there
> Keeps the human soul from care . . .

A vivid meter suits the vividness of the macabre or fantastic :

> Of his bones are coral made;
> Those are pearls that were his eyes:
> Nothing of him that doth fade
> But doth suffer a sea-change
> Into something rich and strange.
> Sea-nymphs hourly ring his knell . . .
>
> . . . .
>
> Round about the cauldron go;
> In the poisoned entrails throw . . .
> Double, double, toil and trouble . . .

Clearly the abundance of trochaic verse in Yeats's later work is partly to be accounted for by the poet's preoccupation with orphic and primitive subjects and by his love of incantatory and epigrammatic tones. All of his dominantly trochaic poems are gnomic or incantatory.[25] In "Mohini Chatterjee" the meter is expressive of the mysterious intensity of the mystic's (and Yeats's own) vision of rebirth and recurrence. In "Under Ben Bulben" Yeats chants as a bard and sage. In "Crazy Jane and the Bishop" the trochaic lines and the trochaic refrain (*All find safety in the tomb*) are as expressive of Jane's macabre wish and imagination as are the cadence refrains (*The solid man and the coxcomb*) and the general raggedness of effect created by the mixing of so many rhythms in one stanza, for the poem's vehemence. Part IV of "Nine-

teen Hundred and Nineteen" is a savage epigram. The poems
on Swift and Alfred Pollexfen are epitaphs of the traditional
mnemonic sort.

Trochaic verse served Yeats in yet another way. In the
manuscripts, and in the published revisions now so conven-
iently available in the Allt and Alspach *Variorum,* one sees
Yeats changing many an iambic line to trochaic—or truncating the iambic, if you will. In "The Two Trees" of the 1895
Poems, for example, the iambic lines

> With broken boughs, and blackened leaves,
> And roots half hidden under snows
> Driven by a storm that ever grieves,

become the trochaic

> That the stormy night receives,
> Roots half hidden under snows,
> Broken boughs and blackened leaves.

One of the most striking instances of this kind of revision is
"The Ballad of the Foxhunter," a poem first collected in
Crossways (1889). The final revision involves quite a number
of lines, and the change in each case is from iambic to trochaic
(or to truncated iambic—the effect is the same). Below I have
juxtaposed several lines from one early version of the poem
(A) with the corresponding lines of the final version (B).
Thomas Parkinson deals with this poem in his fine book *W. B.
Yeats, Self-Critic,*[26] and I am much indebted to him for the
analysis that follows :

Version	Line	
A	1	"Now lay me in a cushioned chair
	2	And carry me, you four . . ."
B	1	"Lay me in a cushioned chair;
	2	Carry me, ye four . . ."
A	7	"And lead him gently in a ring . . ."
B	7	"Lead my Lollard to and fro . . ."
A	9	"Now leave the chair upon the grass . . ."
B	9	"Put the chair upon the grass . . ."

Version	Line	
A	25 & 33	"My huntsman Rody, blow the horn . . ."
B	25 & 33	"Huntsman Rody, blow the horn . . ."
A	29	A fire is in the old man's eyes . . .
B	29	Fire is in the old man's eyes . . .
A	37	The servants round his cushioned place . . .
B	37	Servants round his cushioned place . . .
A	39	And hounds are gazing on his face . . .
B	39	Hounds are gazing on his face . . .
A	40	Both aged hounds and young . . .
B	40	Aged hounds and young . . .

In several instances the change of meter comes about simply as a result of Yeats's lopping off the first word of a line (the poem's monosyllabism made revision easy). In some of the lines it was no doubt these extraneous initial words that Yeats wanted to get rid of, so as to tighten the expression; the resulting trochaic meter is simply a by-product of abridgement. Still, the meter may have been sought for its own sake, too, since it has the advantage of furnishing an interesting counterpoint to the ballad's prevailing iambic meter and the further advantage of giving an added transitiveness and imperative quality to the old hunter's directions. The rhetoric is considerably improved. The pronoun in "My huntsman Rody" is mere padding (and sentimental at that) to make the iambic beat come out right. "A fire is in the old man's eyes" is trite or at best undistinguished; removing the article lights the fire.

And so the trochee served Yeats in various ways. His love of tradition and his devotion to the simpler metrical forms, his love of runic utterance and incantation and terse mnemonic *sententiae*—all this gave him a great call for the measure. It is such an old and celebrated and omnipresent meter that any search for models or influences is pointless. One suspects that it was most strongly recommended to Yeats by the impressive example of Blake, whom he edited. The beloved Swift, too, is perhaps not far away. As we have already seen, Yeats's trochaic couplet poems are often well larded with iambic tetrameter couplets—sometimes it is the iambic that prevails—and the latter was one of the Dean's favorite verse forms. Certainly the atmosphere of "Under Ben Bulben" is much like that of the Augustan's own "Verses on the Death of Dr. Swift." But perhaps all that can be said is that the devotion of two of Yeats's intellectual ancestors to septasyllabic and octosyllabic couplets may well have helped to confirm the Irish poet in his fondness for what are, after all, common measures.

8

Yeats the Rhymer

Rhyme . . . is brave, and generous,
and his dominion pleasing.

—Dryden

FEW OF OUR POETS have loved rhyme as well as Yeats did. For all the experimentalism and modernist tendencies of his mature years, he held insistently onto this one traditional ensign. He kept it up through the heyday of *vers libre,* and after his meetings with Pound, and after so conservative a man as Robert Bridges had decided to abandon it. Yeats's first published poems are rhymed, and all but two of the fifty-seven pieces in *Last Poems* are in rhyme of some sort. Yeats's reputation has not gone down; he is still the great poet nearest us in time; and this is true despite a continuing widespread antipathy to rhyme. The fact in itself is convincing proof that Yeats in nowhere surer than in his rhyming. It never becomes an end in itself, and that is remarkable in a prolific poet who finds it so irresistible.

"The Song of the Happy Shepherd," one of the very earliest poems, rhymes expertly. There are not a few surprises in its music :

> The woods of Arcady are dead,
> And over is their antique joy;
> Of old the world on dreaming fed;
> Grey Truth is now her painted toy;
> Yet still she turns her restless head:
> But O, sick children of the world,
> Of all the many changing things
> In dreary dancing past us whirled,
> To the cracked tune that Chronos sings,
> Words alone are certain good.
> Where are now the warring kings,
> Word be-mockers?—By the rood,
> Where are now the warring kings?

The opening four lines of this part of the poem (1–13) form a logical quatrain, and so one expects to move from one quatrain to another. But the fifth line repeats the *a*-rhyme, carrying the mind back into the quatrain and thus bringing greater unity to the developing thought—and subtlety to the music. Then the same thing—but not quite the same thing— happens again in the next group of lines : this time a *b*-rhyme is repeated again.[27] Similar felicities of variation mark this early poem elsewhere in the first section and in the other two sections as well. Indeed, as is often the case with youthful poetry, the musicianship is superior to diction and quality and progression of thought. Nothing in the poem's versification, for example, is as awkward as the conceptual disharmony of the sequence "*changing* things . . . dreary dancing . . . whirled" in lines seven and eight.

In the mature verse the rhyme does all the things the "generous" device is capable of doing, and very often all of them at once or all in a single poem or stanza. It helps pro- duce that verbal conspicuousness and that instantaneity which are the *sine qua non* of genuine poetry; it firms the individual line; it brings greater coherence to lines that belong together logically; it pulls the attention forward into the stanza, or harks it back to an earlier thought or image; it pleases because we take pleasure in artifice, and pleases by establishing a pattern that continually arouses and then continually satisfies—or surprises—expectations; it increases the emphasis of important words; its melody matches the *cantabile* of feeling, or else it chants a mystery or vision, or hammers home hard images and stark aphorisms; it adds resonance and mnemonic power; and it is absent where it should be absent.

Though Yeats, as we have seen, is no facile or highly experimental metrist, his innovations—it would really be more accurate to call them variations on traditional structures —sometimes result in unusually expressive stanzas. "The Wild Swans at Coole," to take an example rather arbitrarily, will repay the closest analysis of its versification. Certainly the rhyme itself accounts for no small part of this poem's effectiveness :

> The trees are in their autumn beauty,
> The woodland paths are dry,
> Under the October twilight the water
> Mirrors a still sky;
> Upon the brimming water among the stones
> Are nine-and-fifty swans.
>
> The nineteenth autumn has come upon me
> Since I first made my count;
> I saw, before I had well finished,
> All suddenly mount
> And scatter wheeling in great broken rings
> Upon their clamorous wings . . .

This stanza is the only one of its kind in Yeats's work and, as far as I know, in the language. The decision to leave two lines unrhymed and to end them on feminine words is a master stroke. They not only introduce variety; being rhymeless, they decrease aesthetic distance, heighten the impression of informal speech, an impression already established by the poem's chaste and simple diction and ordinary prose syntax. And with the drop in stress and pitch they create, in context, just that touch of dying cadence which suits the expression of a softly meditative and poignant experience. (A similar dying or hushing effect comes at the close of every stanza, where Yeats has shortened the mating lines of his couplet to mere trimeters.) Perhaps Yeats felt that the poem would have become too soft and pat if the unrhymed lines had gone all the way to feminine rhyme. And in Yeats's context there are no conceivable rhymes anyway for "beauty" or "water"—key words, by the way, that need to be just where they are : in places of prominence, out at the ends of the lines. The "water" and "beautiful" that echo them so mysteriously and movingly in the final stanza put rhyme simply out of the question :

> But now they drift on the still water,
> Mysterious, beautiful;
> Among what rushes will they build,
> By what lake's edge or pool
> Delight men's eyes when I awake some day
> To find they have flown away?

The vowel rhymes of the poem's closing couplet enact the sense : the mouth is open in wonder; time and the sky are open to the swans; the length, as well as the sonority of the long vowel, has the right feel for the expanse of time and the conjectured continuing appearances of the swans.

Perhaps the most unusual handling of rhyme in all Yeats is that in the very early poem "Aedh wishes for the Cloths of Heaven," printed in *The Wind Among the Reeds* (1899) and, significantly, one of the few poems Yeats never revised:

> Had I the heavens' embroidered cloths,
> Enwrought with golden and silver light,
> The blue and the dim and the dark cloths
> Of night and light and the half-light,
> I would spread the cloths under your feet:
> But I, being poor, have only my dreams;
> I have spread my dreams under your feet;
> Tread softly because you tread on my dreams.

Yeats never wrote a better lyric than this. Its artistry is perfect, quickening the wholly traditional theme of a young

man's romantic idealism toward his beloved. Standing amongst
a group of poems generally vague, sentimental, and cast in
standard rhymes and uncritically inherited meter, it is fresh
and untouched by sentimentality. It is indeed so perfectly
realized in every detail of expression that it transcends the
theme of young love and strikes home with a more moving,
because more generalized, expression of our capacity to adore
that which is other than the self and beyond the self. The
oddity of the poem's rhyme, of course, is that it is *rime riche*;
to my recollection it is the only instance of such rhyme in
Yeats. It is the kind of triumph that could never be repeated
—or, by an artist both sensitive and prudent (as Yeats was),
even attempted again. Unique as the versification is, however,
one notices that it is also only a little out of Yeats's way. The
form is that of a quatrain (two quatrains are run together),
Yeats's favorite choice in his early years. The effect of the
rime riche is to reduce contrasts in both acoustics and sense, or
looking at it another way, to secure a singleness of mood, a
unity so absolute as to amount to fixation. In many cases *rime
riche* is used in such a way that the poem stands as a mere
metrical curiosity, a virtuoso piece without power or humanity.
But in Yeats's poem the identical rhymes grow organically
out of a veritable tissue of repetition. The poem reminds one,
especially in its second half, of the movement of the Psalms,
the rhythmic effect owing as much to verbal parallelisms as
to the metrical units. Phrase after phrase runs in parallel. And
every other means of securing singleness of design is put to
work : a half dozen of the nouns and verbs are repeated a
total of fifteen times, and the pronoun forms are also re-
iterated; the rhyme words of the second quatrain correspond
by assonance; internal rhyme appears; the quatrains themselves run together as the two close-knit halves of a single
sentence. Though my subject here is the poem's rhyme, I
could not pass on without calling attention to the meter. The
peculiarity is the variation Yeats plays on his stock iambic-
anapestic measure. He works into that basic pattern a number
of deviations, in the form of trochees, spondees, and mono-
syllabic feet, as in

The blue|and the dim|and the dark|cloths

Of night|and light|and the hálf|líght,

and in

I have spread|my dreams|under|your feet;

Tréad sóft|ly because|you tread|on my|dreams.

(The first pair of lines quoted above could also be scanned, of course, as terminating on ionic feet or on pyrrhics followed by spondees. My point, in any case, is the variation from regular dissyllabic rising rhythm.) The result is a fair amount of irregularity; that, in turn, serves to decrease the aesthetic distance normally created by the very conspicuous and dangerous iambic-anapestic meter. The rhythm is thus brought closer to the intimacy and urgency of actual speech. (The suggestion of extemporaneous informal speech inheres, too, of course, in the poem's almost completely Anglo-Saxon diction and straightforward syntax—and, for that matter, in the very repetition of words and phrases.) The unexpected trochees and juxtaposed stresses also chasten the speed and lilt of the iambic-anapestic measure; they introduce a touch of qualities that may be roughly described by words such as hesitation, tentativeness, and apology; and thus they seem to enact the lover's delicacy and deference toward his beloved. The two modes—buoyant feeling and loving tentativeness—coexist in a rich harmony.

Motifs enlivened and woven more richly together by means of rhyme are a constant feature of Yeats's later poetry, especially of the octave pieces, where he again and again reaches the heights of his powers. For example, in "A Prayer for My Daughter," a poem that despite a few blemishes would of itself assure Yeats a place in English poetry, the second couplet of the fifth stanza :

[Hearts are not had as a gift but hearts are earned]
By those that are not entirely beautiful;
Yet many, that have played the fool . . .

picks up and enriches the motifs of the preceding stanza's opening couplet :

> Helen being chosen found life flat and dull
> And later had much trouble from a fool.

The brace couplet of the seventh stanza :

> If there's no hatred in a mind
> Assault and battery of the wind
> [Can never tear the linnet from the leaf] . . .

harks back to phrases in the first stanza : the "roof-levelling wind" and the "great gloom that is in my mind." At the same time this couplet leads on into those lines of the eighth stanza :

> Have I not seen the loveliest woman born
> Out of the mouth of Plenty's horn,
> Because of her opinionated mind
> Barter that horn and every good
> By quiet natures understood
> For an old bellows full of angry wind?

In the ninth stanza comes the resolution, and here it is just right that the rhyme on "howl" should take us back to the poem's opening statement. "Once more the storm is howling" :

> She can, though every face should scowl
> And every windy quarter howl
> Or every bellows burst, be happy still.

And at the close of the poem the eighth stanza's association of ideal loveliness with the fabled cornucopia is developed and clarified :

> How but in custom and in ceremony
> Are innocence and beauty born?
> Ceremony's a name for the rich horn,
> And custom for the spreading laurel tree.

The importance of the resonance—in meaning and music at once—created by such repetitions can scarcely be overestimated. It certainly gives this poem a richness of texture Yeats never surpassed.

Yeats knew how to use rhyme to contribute to the lightest

as well as to the most serious or ecstatic effects. In "For Anne Gregory," a good-natured and even humorous compliment to Lady Gregory's granddaughter and one of the best of the lighter poems, the refrain and the economy of the rhyme (all nine rhymes are keyed on the word "hair") at once strengthen the speaker's argument and create the burden that keeps the yellow hair before our eyes. "High Talk," a sprightly piece that celebrates High Imaginativeness and every artistic extreme and exaggeration that produces lively and lasting pleasure in an audience (and that scorns the drabness and literalism of "machine-shop" realism), enacts its point through the rhyme as much as through the fantastic and raucous imagery, the progressively wilder metaphor, the long lines (prosody on stilts), and the swift irregular rhythm. The rhymes are masculine and are set in couplets (consecutive rhyme is the most emphatic of rhyming patterns); they are followed, in every case, by a caesura; their vowels or diphthongs are long in every case; and in several instances they alliterate or assonate with other nearby words : every means is employed to render the rhymes percussive, and thereby to establish by wit and comedy and plain vigor the poem's point :

Because piebald ponies, led bears, caged lions, make but poor shows,
Because children demand Daddy-long-legs upon his timber toes,
Because women in the upper storeys demand a face at the pane,
That patching old heels they may shriek, I take to chisel and plane . . .

Surveying Yeats's rhyme as a whole, one notices (particularly in the later poems) two peculiarities : there is a great deal of slant rhyme and very little feminine rhyme (*un*rhymed feminine endings are also rare). The existence of the slant rhyme poses interesting and somewhat complicated problems that will require an extended discussion. The paucity of feminine rhyme in the poetry Yeats wrote from 1910 or so onward seems to me to be more easily explained. It is indeed a paucity. I doubt that there is another body of English poetry (comparable in size and quality, and Pope excepted) that shows so little of it. The fact would not be remarkable in an age which (like the Augustan) generally proscribed feminine rhyme (in serious verse). But like the Elizabethans, the free-reined Romantics and their heirs thought well of the feminine ending, rhymed or unrhymed. The Anglo-Irish tradition —the whole of it, from the early lyrics and ballads to contemporaries of Yeats like Joseph Campbell, Oliver Gogarty, and Katharine Tynan—certainly shows no aversion to it. Its scarcity in Yeats (once he is out of his early years) follows, I believe, from his serious and dignified cast of mind and particularly from his growing determination to give his verse a texture that would accommodate hard and compact thought and hard beauty and passionateness. The feminine ending, which trails downward anticlimactically and which, when rhymed, has the added disadvantage of being conspicuous as well as weak, found little place in such an ambition. In those rare lines in the later poems where feminine rhyme does occur, however, it seems unexceptionable. In "A Prayer for My Daughter," for example, there are feminine couplets in the sixth and ninth stanzas, and in both instances the movement into the lighter, more melodic rhyme is perfectly appropriate: these are the lightest and sweetest moments in the whole poem —pure serene song.

As Yeats matured, he grew more and more fond of slant rhyme. In fact, it became a characteristic of his verse, a mark of the Yeatsian style (though never a mannerism). He used it more extensively than any English poet before him, and though a few lesser and more recent poets have used it even more pervasively, probably no one has used it so aptly. The reasons for his success with it are, I think, clear and profoundly interesting.

In the first place, he evolved rather than manufactured it. With him it does not have that smell of the lamp, or the worse smell of a doctrinaire and desperate originality that it so often has in the hands of poets who have made it a fashionable badge of modernity, and hence a cliché rather than an organ of solid, unpretentious art. Yeats began to take it up because he was both ripe for it and in need of it. Few of his successors in slant rhyme have previously mastered ordinary rhyme, and the difference is telling. Yeats's ear, attuned to the finest nuances of traditional rhyme, knew when and just how to roughen the harmony. And he knew the liabilities with the assets. As a matter of fact, he never once risked—and I hope to show that a great risk is involved—a whole poem in slant rhyme.

There is of course a sprinkling of imperfect rhyme even in the early poetry, but no more (or little more) than one expects in traditional English verse. Most of what little there is may be termed conventional license (and of course some of the pairings that are imperfect by king's-English standards are perfect, or close to being perfect, in one or another species of Irish English). There is the traditional rhyming of "love" with "move," "rove," and "grove," of "multitude" and "solitude" with words like "good" and "wood." In *The Rose* (1893) there is "good" with "mood" in "A Cradle Song," "wood" with "solitude" and "words" with "boards" in "A Dream of Death," and "wars" with "cars" (a true rhyme generally in Irish English) in "Cuchulain's Fight with the Sea." Beginning with *The Green Helmet and Other Poems* (1910) slant rhyme is ubiquitous. And one must now call it slant rhyme. There is no way to get the "difficult" and "jolt" or the "blood" and "cloud" of "The Fascination of What's Difficult," the "thumb" and "became" of "The Tower" (II), or the "obstacle" and "hill" of "A Prayer for My Daughter" to make perfect rhyme, whether you are from Leinster or Leicester, Dungarvan or Dover. Slant rhyme abounds in *Last Poems*. About half the rhyme of "The Gyres," the first poem in that volume, is muted. Here are the rhyme words (imperfect rhymes italicized):

> *forth* worth earth
> *thought* out about
> Troy joy
> top drop *up*
> *stain* *gone* *again*
> voice rejoice
> *Soul* *shall* *all*
> *dear* sepulchre disinter
> *run* again

"The Municipal Gallery Revisited" shows a similar abundance of slanted rhymes. Here is its third stanza :

> Heart-smitten with emotion I sink down,
> My heart recovering with covered eyes;
> Wherever I had looked I had looked upon
> My permanent or impermanent images:
> Augusta Gregory's son; her sister's son,
> Hugh Lane, 'onlie begetter' of all these;
> Hazel Lavery living and dying, that tale
> As though some ballad-singer had sung it all.

In this stanza there is not a single pure rhyme, even after making allowances for Irish pronunciations. It is an extreme case, but slant rhyme dominates many of the poems almost as heavily. "The Statues," "News for the Delphic Oracle," "Long-Legged Fly," "Crazy Jane on the Mountain," the *terza rima* poem "Cuchulain Comforted," and the closing poem and epitaph, "Under Ben Bulben," are especially full of it. The last-named poem opens with slant-rhyme couplets :

> Swear by what the sages spoke
> Round the Mareotic Lake
> That the Witch of Atlas knew,
> Spoke and set the cocks a-crow.

The conclusion (Part VI), up to the epitaph itself, is cast wholly in slant rhyme : *head, laid / there, near / cross, phrase / spot, cut.*

It is insupportable, I think, to hold that in every instance Yeats deliberately chose his imperfect rhyme to achieve special effects that could not have been rendered by ordinary rhyme One must sometimes remember the very valuable principle that in a work of art things are often as they are simply because they are not inappropriate that way. No doubt in many cases Yeats was just unable to find a full rhyme that suited the context as well as the partial harmony on which he finally decided. His rigorous determination, in his maturity, to suffer nothing to take precedence over packed thought and observation which would be expressed as passionately as in the best of the Metaphysicals, forces us to regard the quantity of imperfect rhyme as in part the absolute subservience of prosody to substance. Undoubtedly, too, Yeats, like many another poet, must have tired at times of consistently regular rhyme and in some cases taken to muting it (where another poet might take up free or blank verse) for the relief of a jaded ear.

He had other needs that slant rhyme could meet. It ministered, I believe, to his increasing willingness to express dissonant feeling and to his compulsion to celebrate, with Blake and Lawrence, passion—including fury and hatred—for its own sake. In general the slant rhyme seems to be a prosodic correlative of Yeats's propensity for scorn and hatred, of his romantic sympathy with rusticity and earthiness and craziness, and of his late fascination with the cruder aspects of sexuality. The point is worth pursuing further.

Imperfect rhyme is a matter of sounds almost, but not quite, mating. The phonological effect is one of incomplete resolution, or dissonance (I assume, of course, a reader who is sensitive to timbre and rhythm). And this effect is what makes slant rhyme so appropriate for verse that expresses conditions like tension, anxiety, and anguish. The acoustic dissonance helps establish the point of experiential dissonance. And of course the presence of the disharmonious feeling as subject matter makes us all the more aware of the discordant music (the principle here is that meaning activates and channels the suggestive or enactive potential of verbal sounds; quantities of proximate voiceless *s*'s in a context that deals with the hissing of vipers will seem onomatopoeic, but the same sounds could never in any circumstance render a physical suggestion of, say, the booming of drums or the moan of doves). All this is to say that in the appropriate context slant rhyme can help vivify qualities of feeling that lie within the general areas of difficulty and pain. In fact, imperfect rhyme always produces a certain discordance (though it may be very slight, mitigated by such conditions as enjambment, alternation of rhyme, and word euphony) regardless of context. And that is one reason why it so easily becomes a highly self-conscious element. It irritates us, so to speak, and so tends to draw attention to itself as artifice. It tends to throw enormous emphasis (the greatest emphasis, I believe, that it is possible to obtain in English rhyme) upon the meshing words. The whole tendency is to violate the desire of art to conceal itself. Only a fine poet can manage, without banality, consistent terminal emphasis.

This kind of rhyme is all the more self-conscious because it comes unexpected. Historically speaking, there is no tradition of it (or only a thin and very recent tradition) in English. And of course we do not—could not if we wanted to—read poetry in a vacuum. When confronted with persistent or conspicuous slant rhyme, we may ask for justification—and this is not an afterthought but really a part of our aesthetic experience: "Why this variance from ordinary rhyme?" If we find that nothing in the poem is complemented by the muted (and now all too loud!) rhyme, or if the contest will not support the unusual degree of terminal emphasis, we judge the poem to be flawed: we are not satisfied that form and matter have been perfectly blended, we are not drawn into an imaginative experience as deeply as we might be but tend to recoil, questioning, mistrusting (and the fourth reading, when all's clear and response judicious, will be no better than the first); the work may possess merit, but it is bound to yield to the imagination only an imperfect pleasure.

Yeats avoids such perils by using slant rhyme not as a norm but as a more than occasional variant and by avoiding long stretches of slant-rhymed couplets, the form that renders the dissonance and emphasis most powerfully. Take, for example, the stanza quoted above from "The Municipal Gallery Revisited." One scarcely notices that the rhyme is "off." The ear may catch the false couplet (*tale, all*) at once, but the alternation of the rhymes elsewhere diminishes their conspicuousness; also there is no strident feeling to alert the ear to dissonance; and the somewhat proselike (yet elevated) quality of the lines—a product of irregular meter, prose diction and syntax, proper nouns, and a tone of reminiscence— leads one not to anticipate conspicuous rhyme (as one does in song or incantation)—the overall effect is very nearly that of blank verse. In this stanza, as in many others, Yeats does not seem to be employing slant rhyme as a special device; it would seem that he merely ran out of suitable rhyme words, or tired of rhyme, or simply and not unwisely did not insist on it. There can be no quarrel with the result.

The slant rhymes of "To a Friend Whose Work Has Come to Nothing" (a poem for which even Yvor Winters, no lover of Yeats, has found some praise) lend vigor to the speaker's exhortations of his beleaguered friend (Lady Gregory) and to his scorn for every "brazen throat" (the philistine Irish rabble). The rhymes that are not slanted are not particularly euphonious. Conjoined with the plain wording, the terse style, and the rather irregular meter, the rhyme produces a timbre that seems an acoustic emblem of frankness and moral vigor. Yeats withholds, under the circumstances, any tranquilizer and offers instead a tonic. Lady Gregory's work on behalf of the controversial Dublin art gallery proposed by Hugh Lane has borne bitter fruit; further effort at the time is meaningless and worse; *noblesse* is not mere form but a quality of soul that can keep or strengthen its tone only by drawing back from contests with unworthy opponents.

The slant rhyme of "Under Ben Bulben" is similarly effective, adding sinew to this last will and testament. The imperfect rhyme is particularly fitting in the conclusion : "No marble, no conventional phrase"—and here no conventional rhyme.

Yeats's late preoccupation with lust and direct sexual pleasure endears him to many a modern spirit and provokes the contempt—by no means always a prudish or ignorant response—of others. However, few readers will argue that Yeats is at his best in that body of poetry. With only a handful of exceptions his greatest poems are meditative and reminiscing pieces, surprisingly often cast in octave stanzas. Yeats's literary fascination with raw sex, however, does figure as prominently in the later poetry as the mysticism of the visionary or the moving reverie of the aging and reflective artist and responsible public man. The sharply erotic verse is by no means confined to "Leda and the Swan," the Crazy Jane poems, and the pieces of *A Woman Young and Old*. And this poetry is generally full of slant rhyme, and one often feels that here the device is expressive. In the fourth section of "Under Ben Bulben," Michael Angelo's "half-awakened Adam," excites "globe-trotting Madam"

> Till her bowels are in heat,
> Proof that there's a purpose set.

And in "News for the Delphic Oracle"

> Peleus on Thetis stares . . .
> Love has blinded him with tears

and

> Belly, shoulder, bum,
> Flash fishlike; nymphs and satyrs
> Copulate in the foam.

The slant rhyme seems to help intensify the sexual image or idea—perhaps through a slight suggestion of unresolved desire (from the unresolved chord of the rhyme) or of half-pleasing inflammation (from the irritation of prosodic dissonance). In positing this effect of Yeats's imperfect rhyme in bluntly sexual contexts I am trying not to exaggerate the expressive power of verbal sound; and I am not trying to be clever-deep in the approved Modernist way. I can only report my own experience, gained from readings of Yeats long before I possessed any theory (or much knowledge) of metrics and continually confirmed thereafter; and I have good reason not to think my response unique or unusual.

I want to close with a quite unverified (and probably unverifiable) speculation. It seems to me that Yeats's attraction to slant rhyme was partly a result of his living in a country where almost all the English was Irish English of one sort or another. Yeats was unquestionably aware of the dialectal differences. He knew that many of his rhymes, regular enough in one pronunciation, would be irregular in another. His own pronunciation (which was essentially Received Standard English) does not by any means settle everything; quite the contrary. He wrote, as I say, conscious of Standard and Sligo, of Galway peasant and Dublin educated—and with allegiances to all; and so in no few instances the question of his rhyme is obscurely—and richly—relative. The argument for this notion is, first of all, that such a state of tension exactly suited Yeats's dual cultural allegiance—it was natural, a path of little resistance—and, secondly, that this particular linguistic eclecticism or ambiguity suits Yeats's overall eclecticism of subject and mood and his well-known desire not to have the meanings of any of his poems limited by some "final" interpretation. The chief argument against the conjecture is, I suppose, the lack of any explicit confirmation in Yeats's writings or authenticated remarks (at least I have never noticed any such references in my own perusals). But that Yeats may have enjoyed an unconscious relish here seems to me perfectly plausible.

Finally, one suspects that William Blake may be nearby. Blake used slant rhyme boldly, and Yeats was his editor; and Blake's father was John O'Neill of Dublin and London.

I have not yet tried to answer the most interesting question of all: why is Yeats so very fond of rhyme in one form or another?

Despite the scarcity of English rhyme words (especially of those that can be brought together with both sense and dignity!) and the prestige of blank verse (and more recently of free verse), our poets still inherit a tradition that bids them rhyme unless there be good reason not to. Rhymer after rhymer has railed against the "fetter" and the "jingle." But whether their animadversions reflect the classical bias and the momentary fit of impatience of a Jonson or Milton or the fanatic polemicizing of a William Carlos Williams, English poetry has a way of settling back into rhyme. Our lyric poetry seems particularly dependent upon it. It is not indispensable even in the very shortest and most intense lyrics; but one has difficulty conceiving of a great body of English lyric verse achieving the richest resonance or most haunting power without it.

In any event, English poetry (including that written in Ireland) was still a rhyming poetry in the 1880's when Yeats began to write, and Yeats—a lyricist, like almost all young poets—far from being a great rebel with a passion for radical innovations in metrics (or other matters), was a lover of received things. Then, too, he was even more of an aesthete than is usually the case with sensitive young men, and so the music and the architectonic possibilities of rhyme were immediately attractive to him. His family background and his years of boyhood and young manhood—they were unhurried and rather undirected, and many of them were spent in lonely pastoral places of beauty haunted by a vigorously imaginative tradition—brought his innate aestheticism to the fore. Yeats grew up in the midst of his father's and brother's paintings, and for a while he contributed his own. Somewhat ironically, the radical rationalism of the father, which so dismayed the son, drove the young romantic all the more deeply into aesthetic pleasures and the cultivation of mystery. It is also true that late or soon, and for a host of reasons, many poets who begin as lyricists find that their main ability or interest lies in narrative or explicitly philosophical verse or in drama —genres to which an unrhymed measure of some sort is likely to prove congenial. Often, too, poets come to love more and more the virtues of that "other harmony"—the logic, the detail, the flexibility, the realistic and humble registers, the relaxation, it allows. And Orpheus at fifty, the master craftsman, may want to see how well he can perform with the fewest possible technical advantages. If nothing more, he may tire of the sounding charm. No one should find it a mystery that a poet begins to look askance at rhyme.

Yeats, however, despite his permutations, remained a rhymer; and again both disposition and circumstance played their parts. In the first place, the Irish tradition, from the times of Mève and Finn mac Cool to those of Synge and O'Casey, is a tradition of song and lyric narrative, not an ethical or speculative tradition. Yeats loved that tradition and in the main wanted to work within it. By birth, temperament, and historical moment he is, of course, much more philosophical and cosmopolitan than the old Celtic genius. He is of England as well as "of Ireland," and he is of the shrunken

modern world. He is inevitably a modern and to some extent
a "poet of ideas." But Yeats detested "the literature of the
point of view." He had an enormous aversion to many aspects
of modernism and particularly of hypercerebralism—to super-
rationalism, superplanning, ideation become a Gorgon at
which the heart and the imagination dare not look. He cultivated his ready empathy with the hand-crafted and slow-
moving past, where peasant, aristocrat, and artist created
beautiful stories, beautiful manners, and beautiful art. "Traditional sanctity and loveliness" was a beauty not capable of
being produced, or perhaps even preserved, in the modern
world, where "all's Whiggery . . . a levelling, rancorous,
rational sort of mind." Possessing an inward eye as keen as
his outward eyes were remiss and untrained, he also cultivated
theosophical methods of inducing a state of consciousness
favorable to the formation of vivid images, and so found in
"magic," too, some release from the mechanistic, abstracting
habit of mind out of which arise so many of the values of
modernism. (This relative ease of conjuring images, together
with his intuitive grasp of the kinds of images that would
serve to symbolize evocatively passions and aspirations and
phases of history, makes many of the symbols he devised for
his private mythology seem as spontaneous and act upon the
imagination as powerfully as those of Spenser and Shakespeare.) Yeats's seemingly inborn hatred of Whiggery was
strongly abetted by his early reaction against his father's
rationalism.

One should notice also that Yeats became, and was delighted to become, an occasional poet par excellence. He may
have dwelt, as Arland Ussher says, in a "world of phantoms,"
but he was also the poet of indignation at theater scandals, of
eulogies and ironies for Irish national leaders, of grieving for
dead (or atrophied) companions and heroes, of *sententiae* for
floundering friends or second-rate imitators. Here the short
poem is called for—the lyric, the lyric meditation, the epigram—and all these cry out for rhyme.

No doubt Yeats's romantic idealism also helped keep him a
rhymer. Time after time, even in his later years, his subject is

> whatever most can bless
> The mind of man or elevate a rhyme.

Physical and moral beauty—swans and Maude Gonne, Connolly and Robert Gregory; charm of refined person and serene place—Lady Gregory and Dorothy Wellesley, Coole Park and Lissadell; pride in craftsmanship and in heritage; visions of the heroic spirit, of the unity of being, of the immortal and perfected soul—Fergus and Cuchulain, Byzantium, the golden bird; above all, Romance—"high courtesy" and "the old high way of love" and "radical innocence" and "players and painted stage" : these are themes that welcome rhyme. For rhyme, as Henry Lanz has demonstrated persuasively,[28] creates musical pleasure. The mating sounds create an acoustic effect which in turn creates a quality of feeling that is to some degree independent of context and that may be indicated roughly by words such as charm, sweetness, resolution, harmony. And it is not only this musical aspect of rhyme that would have appealed strongly to Yeats. Rhyme has also a ritualistic or liturgical aspect; it orders and formalizes, and this order or pattern has in itself an expressive value that couuld not have been lost on Yeats, whose Burkean and Nietzschean hatred of mob restiveness, of Whiggery and "mere anarchy," and—on the positive side—whose deeply romantic and aristocratic love of custom and ceremony, and whose devotion to the Protestant Ascendancy, were boundless. The best case—a massive and brilliant one—for the affinity between rhyme and a romantic and conservative (or merely conservative) temperament is to be found in Lanz's book. This notion does not ask one to ignore the possibility of aesthetic conservatism (or tight artistic discipline) coexisting with political liberalism or neoterism (Bertolt Brecht is a rhymer, too); it only points out the fact that generally (in the western world, in modern times, and in languages where rhyme has had some standing) the relatively settled or placid periods and the poets who are political conservatives have found a special attractiveness in rhyme.[29]

What is less open to debate or qualification, of course, is that Yeats's reluctance to abandon rhyme, even after he had come to relish very great metrical freedom, and keys near those of prose, argues for his good sense : he knew and never forgot that rhyming verse was his instinct and his mastered trade.

9

Idealized Speech

All must be an idealization of speech. . . .
—Reveries Over Childhood
and Youth (1914)

THE EPIGRAPH at the head of this chapter is Yeats's description
of his father's ideal in poetry, but in the Irish poet's mature
years it also came to be his own aspiration. Poetry—lyric and
dramatic poetry, at least—should be idealized speech, recon-
ciling the opposites of talk and song, spontaneity and artifice,
ordinariness and elevation.

Such an idiom, Yeats came to believe, would permit expression of the whole man and make its appeal to the whole
man. One would not be forced into some narrow choice:
thinking or feeling, judiciousness or spontaneity, noble sentiment or earthy humor, the vision or the barb. It would be a
dramatic, engaging poetics because it promised an aesthetic
tension and richness: juxtaposing colloquialisms against inverted word order, and Byzantium and God's holy fire against

a scarecrow. It could carry plain diction and prose syntax in a rhymed and metered stanza. It could commence with a plain, straightforward, terse assertion right out of prose or laconic speech :

> That is no country for old men . . .

and proceed at once to a verbal texture too rich, condensed, symbolic, and elevated for ordinary speech or for prose itself:

>   The young
> In one another's arms, birds in the trees
> —Those dying generations—at their song,
> The salmon-falls, the mackerel-crowded seas,
> Fish, flesh, or fowl, commend all summer long
> Whatever is begotten, born, and dies.

It could take a traditional theme—say, the relative claims of art and life upon our attention—and a traditional verse form—linked quatrains, perhaps—and make its point in a manner at once bizarre and humorous, macabre and anecdotal, obscure and, in its colloquial diction and loosened meter, easygoing, as Yeats does in the 1912 poem "The Dolls," one of the earliest instances of the complete realization of his new aim :

> A doll in the doll-maker's house
> Looks at the cradle and bawls:
> "That is an insult to us."
> But the oldest of all the dolls,
> Who had seen, being kept for show,
> Generations of his sort,
> Outscreams the whole shelf . . .

It was hardly a new ideal in English or in Irish English poetry, but it was novel for Yeats (and of course for all the dwellers in the Pre-Raphaelite and Celtic twilights); it meant that he would have to work hard to get away from the main drift of his early poetry, which was a rather sentimental idealism. In 1913 in a letter to his father Yeats said that of late he had been trying to make his work "convincing with a speech so natural and dramatic that the hearer would feel the presence of a man thinking and feeling."[30] And later, along the same lines: "I tried to make the language of poetry coincide with that of passionate, normal speech."[31] Such comments could be multiplied from the mature poet's essays and letters. And yet it is wrong to think of Yeats as moving in a straight or nearly straight line away from romance and heroic exaltation and rhyme and meter toward realism and casualism and cadence and speech locution. His interest in the artifices of verse never dies. A majority of the most impressive poems of his later years are written in difficult and rather elaborate octave stanzas (including the *ottava rima*). All but a handful of the poems of his final decade rhyme; many are cast in the same deftly irregular iambic verse he had mastered a quarter of a century earlier. The meter of "The Municipal Gallery Revisited" (a poem written in the autumn of 1937):

> Wherever I had looked I had looked upon
> My permanent or impermanent images . . .

might have been written two decades earlier: it is the same tone and the same relaxed iambic line one finds in the rich and moving poem "In Memory of Major Robert Gregory" (1917):

> I had thought, seeing how bitter is that wind
> That shakes the shutter, to have brought to mind
> All those that manhood tried, or childhood loved . . .

The tension, the rhythmic richness of words and phrases pulling against the regular pattern of the measure, exercises a perennial fascination. Yeats had no thought of abandoning one good for another when he saw that he could have both. The attraction metrical freedom held for him as he matured never became strong enough to bring him over to *vers libre*. He never once abandons both rhyme and meter in a poem, though in a very few cases he comes close to doing that. The poem cast in a traditional framework but full of cadence and actual speech locutions is the typical poem of his last three decades; and the kind of poem that is not written in stanzas, but in irregular sections, that shows no regular pattern of line-length or of rhyme, and that often incorporates a great deal of cadence, is by no means rare ("The Dawn," "A Thought from Propertius," "Broken Dreams," and "A Crazed Girl" are such poems).

"Cadence" and "speech cadence" are perhaps ambiguous terms, or terms with a history of equivocation. By "cadence" I mean lines of poetry, or portions of lines, that will not (and were not intended to) analyze into feet or other symmetrical components, that have broken entirely out of all metrical framework. For example, lines like these, which occur in basically iambic pentameter poems :

Rooted in one dear perpetual place . . .

Ravening, raging, and uprooting, that he may come . . .

Sometimes the effect is simply that of freedom, and sometimes the qualities of informal speech are strongly suggested; the most typical effect, however, seems to me that of passionate but still somewhat studied and not infrequently declamatory speech. In such constructions intense feeling is always storming the barriers of metrical artifice, impatient with neatness; yet the barriers strain more often than they break, and they almost never break completely.

This prosodic ideal springs directly, of course, from Yeats's view of poetry itself. "Idealized speech" implies in a phrase Yeats's lifelong fascination with the extremes of human experience and the reconciliation of opposites. The world is real; so is the golden bird; both lay valid claims on us; to reject either claim is to be less than whole. The golden bird sings in measure; life in its glorious moments bursts out in passionate action and speech. Poetry itself—the greatest poetry, at least— is an art of balance and implies a degree of balance in the poet. It looks toward sheer artistry and musical pleasure and at the same time toward sober thought and rectified feeling, toward perception for the sensuous delight of perceiving, but also for understanding and ordering our experience. At any given moment a "movement" in poetry or the "period" of a particular poet or the drift of a particular poem will threaten to look wholly one way: and so we have poetry turning into ethic, polemic, and philosophy, or into mere *poésie pure.* Yeats is a great poet : he effects the difficult, delicate reconciliation and does so frequently. In "A Prayer for My Daughter" we have the particularity and immediacy of the storm and the lovely song-sheltering trees, but also a prayer for values— innocence, *noblesse,* love of what lives quietly and beautifully and long. Yeats is of the great tradition in perceiving that it is this richness or tension that accounts for no small part of poetry's universal and eternal appeal : it is a verbal mode we have evolved to satisfy just this need for equipoise, and only the charlatan or the innocent will want to turn it into prose or play or philosophy. One feels in Yeats's verse the form-straining pressure of conviction and intense and varied feeling, as one does not feel it in the verse of, say, Oscar Wilde; and yet he does not sacrifice artistry and fall into the bathos of a Carl Sandburg.

To turn again to my stipulations : I would call *Leaves of Grass* cadenced poetry; characteristically it is so oratorical in manner, so full of parallelism, syntactical inversions, verbal idiosyncrasies, terminal caesuras, and other marks which distinguish it alike from ordinary speech and from prose, that one is not tempted to call it "speech cadence." The voice one hears is, for all its gusto, quite literary, stylized (even, in many places, badly mannered, it seems to me). By contrast, much of the free verse of William Carlos Williams is in a humbler register and suggests, where it does not actually incorporate, the diction, the rhythms, the syntax of daily spoken American generally and New Jersey seaboard particularly. This I would call a body of speech-cadenced poetry. Of course, cadence and speech cadence easily and imperceptibly glide into each other, and both forms create the effect of metrical liberty and diminished aesthetic distance.

Yeats's late poem "A Crazed Girl" is cadenced poetry. Although two or three lines of this poem (the last, for example : "O sea-starved, hungry sea") may be interpreted as loose iambic, there is no iambic norm in the poem as a whole. But neither is the metrical irregularity of the sort that suggests familiar, extemporaneous speech. The rhetoric is elevated, formal, despite the liberties :

> That crazed girl improvising her music,
> Her poetry, dancing upon the shore,
> Her soul in division from itself
> Climbing, falling, she knew not where. . . .

In "Crazy Jane on the Mountain" the metrical irregularities do suggest, in places, raw speech:

> I am tired of cursing the Bishop,
>   (Said Crazy Jane)
> Nine books or nine hats
> Would not make him a man.
> I have found something worse
> To meditate on.

The final stanza of "The Circus Animals' Desertion" illustrates clearly the combining of relaxed metrical lines and lines of speech cadence :

> Those masterful images because complete
> Grew in pure mind, but out of what began?
> A mound of refuse or the sweepings of a street,
> Old kettles, old bottles, and a broken can,
> Old iron, old bones, old rags, that raving slut
> Who keeps the till. Now that my ladder's gone,
> I must lie down where all the ladders start,
> In the foul rag-and-bone shop of the heart.

The first three lines here are fairly regular iambic (the third line is a hexameter; the first line may be scanned as beginning with an iambic and then an anapestic foot, or with two iambic feet, the second of which contains an elided syllable). And they are somewhat rhetorical, especially the first two. The next five lines, however, are quite colloquial, and the fourth breaks out of the metrical frame and becomes a line of speech cadence faintly haunted by the iambic ghost (the eighth line, too, almost breaks away). The fifth line is as colloquial as any of the others; it sounds like unretouched, vigorous, extemporaneous utterance, and yet one also feels the iambic undercurrent distinctly.

The same technique of medley may be seen clearly and in a highly successful form in one of Yeats's best light lyrics, the short, opening section—in itself a complete little irony—of *A Woman Young and Old*:

Father and Child

> She hears me strike the board and say
> That she is under ban
> Of all good men and women,
> Being mentioned with a man
> That has the worst of all bad names;
> And thereupon replies
> That his hair is beautiful,
> Cold as the March wind his eyes.

Here the first six lines are distinctly iambic (line three has a feminine ending, line four treats "Being" as a monosyllable—a frequent practice in Yeats and in many other poets). Then there is a two-line paraphrase of the girl's reply, the first line showing speech cadence, the second (with its poetic syntax) mere cadence.[32] Both lines are masterful: their rhythm (loose and sharply contrasting with the rhythm that comes before) makes us feel the daughter's presence and vivifies her moony adolescent ecstasy (a loose feeling that must break the bonds of metrical convention). The father's moral and metrical order naught availeth.

Let us take the whole of another short poem, "A Prayer for Old Age":

> God guard me from those thoughts men think
> In the mind alone;
> He that sings a lasting song
> Thinks in a marrow-bone;
>
> From all that makes a wise old man
> That can be praised of all;
> O what am I that I should not seem
> For the song's sake a fool?
>
> I pray—for fashion's word is out
> And prayer comes round again—

> That I may seem, though I die old,
> A foolish, passionate man.

Some of the lines are regular iambic : 5, 9, 10, 11. Some are trochaic or truncated iambic : 2, 3. Others are as obviously cadence or speech cadence or very loose iambic : 1, 8, 12. Notice the opening line. The natural phrase pattern—in what would seem to be the most obvious, least idiosyncratic reading —is this :

> God guard me|from those thoughts|men think

and the metrical pattern is perhaps this (some readers will prefer to put a full stress on "God" and "men") :

> God guard|me from|those thoughts|men think.

The natural phrasing and stress weights are at odds with the theoretical pattern of iambic tetrameter, though a metrical stress on "from" makes the line suddenly an almost normal iambic one, beneath the hovering cadences of speech.

The early poems of Yeats show few, perhaps no, clear instances of cadence. They do show a certain liking for mixed types of feet within the line (especially iambic and anapestic) and for lines of varying lengths throughout the stanza; and although (as we have seen) ballads and other quatrain forms dominate, there is in fact quite a variety of stanza forms. The inventive ear and the taste for variety and liberty look forward to the far greater inventiveness and freedom that lay ahead. Consider, for example, the meter of "He Thinks of Those Who Have Spoken Evil of His Beloved," a short poem from *The Wind Among the Reeds* (1899) :

> Half close|your eye|lids, loos|en your hair,
> And dream|about|the great|and their pride;
> They have spo|ken against|you eve|rywhere,
> But weigh|this song|with the great|and their pride;
> I made|it out|of a mouth|ful of air,
> Their chil|dren's chil|dren shall say|they have lied.

Every line (the first is a special case) shows four strong beats and four metrical units. But the lines also show two meters, iambic and anapestic. The poem begins on a hovering accent. Degree of stress varies; for example, "out" in line five does not carry nearly as much force as "-lids" in line one. The second and third lines are unlike in both number and order of feet; and the last three lines, while they agree with one another metrically (two iambs are followed by two anapests), obtain a certain liberty from the triple counterpoint of words, phrase, and foot. The poem is in many ways, too, an epitome of Yeats's prime values and a foreshadowing of his later styles. It celebrates the heroic past and values a heroic and aristocratic temper in the present. It stakes all on the magic power of poetry: the suasive beauty of the poem itself will set future judgment right about the lady. The piece is dramatic in technique (direct address) and bold in attitude—many readers will find it even a bit histrionic, as Yeats all too frequently is. The tone is romantic and elevated (behind it lies the untried idealism of the young); at the same time it has nothing of a Shelleyan remoteness. The simple diction and direct word order look forward to the poet who will become the master of the colloquial touch. The brevity and confidence look forward to the epigrammatist. The strong and thrice-repeated rhymes and the repeated key phrase prefigure the incantatory verse to come.

Yeats never complained about the traditional accentual-syllabic line. If there is a disparagement of rhymes or iambs anywhere in his writings, it has escaped my notice. His increasing attraction to cadence and highly irregular iambic meter is the acquiring of new instruments, not the abandoning of the older ones. His rhymeless poems show some sort of meter, and the poems in which the metrical pattern is faint show some kind of rhyme. In any given poem he is willing to sacrifice some, but not all, of the traditional prosodic elements. Rhyme and meter are the necessary concomitants of the values Yeats held, the tones he loved, the effects he sought. He himself gives us, in one of his very rare comments on prosody, lucid reasons for his refusal to take up any *vers libre*. In the unused 1937 "General Introduction for My Work" he objects to the directly autobiographical tendency of free verse, to its proximity to ego and unselected experience. The disciplining, refining, and objectifying powers of determinate form were, he says, desirable and even necessary for him :

> Pound, Turner, Lawrence wrote admirable free verse, I could not. I would lose myself, become joyless like those mad old women. . . . All that is personal soon rots; it must be packed in ice or salt. . . . If I wrote of personal love or sorrow in free verse, or in any rhythm that left it unchanged, amid all its accidence, I would be full of self-contempt because of my egotism and indiscretion, and foresee the boredom of my reader. I must choose a traditional stanza, even what I alter must seem traditional.[33]

Later in the same Introduction he explicitly confirms an attitude which permeates his poetry itself and which is everywhere so generally evident as to stand in no need of such overt confirmation : he identifies meter with the public or popular character of poetry, believing (rightly, if history be a safe guide) that a perceptibly regular measure is usually necessary to poetry which is to transcend coteries and periods and find an audience in every age. It may be at once simpler and more inclusive to say that Yeats associates meter with the past and the past with poetry. To cut himself off from meter, the "ghostly voice," is to cut himself off from the great tradition: "If I repeat the first line of *Paradise Lost* so as to emphasize its five feet I am among the folk singers. . . . What moves me and my hearer is a vivid speech that has no laws except that it must not exorcise the ghostly voice."[34]

From Yeats's perspective free verse was at best too modernist, at worst a symptom of casualism, blurry democratic ecumenism, and hatred of degrees and distinctions. It has indeed acquired a demonstrable coloration of politics, of modern "movements." In the twenties and thirties vast quantities of inartistic and often wondrously bathetic proletarian propaganda were being turned out in a verse very free indeed. It seemed then, as now, the favorite mode of many "progressive" and antitraditional forces in literature and politics. There were also, of course, fascists and people of quasi-facist persuasion (most notably Pound) writing free verse; and the Imagist free verse program was in fact largely aesthetic and nonpolitical. But Yeats was far more of a Burkean conservative and Swiftian aristocrat than he ever was a fascist.[35] His sympathy for Italian and German fascism (about their real character he knew very little) was no doubt greater than his sympathy for bolshevism (about which, in my opinion, he had greater factual knowledge and truer intuitive understanding); but he could not long have looked with favor on any twentieth-century totalitarianism. His espousal of O'Duffy's Blue Shirts was motivated more by chagrin and despair than by natural gravitation; it was brief, and his rejection was absolute. His initial commitment means only that he was desperate and that he was a poet—*l'uomo entusiastico*.

Finally, one might say that for free verse, for "playing tennis with the nets down," Yeats was not only too much of the old school but also too much the aesthete, the lover of form and nuance, and too much the lover of the file and the difficulty overcome. Curiously and fortunately, he was too little the aesthete, too responsible and philosophical and eclectic, to be beguiled by Imagism, most of whose products he found—as we find them today—rather thin.

From what I have said so far, the reader will see that I think it a mistake to conclude that Yeats's experiments with metrical freedom and speech cadence are evidence of an increasing deference to the modern spirit, perhaps initiated or crystallized by his acquaintance with Ezra Pound. It is also dangerous, in my opinion, to consider these prosodic tendencies of Yeats as support for the theory, held even by some wise and conservative writers (by Yeats's friend Robert Bridges, for example), which maintains that the traditional iambic line is "bankrupt." Rather I would say that Yeats's increasing freedom places him the more clearly in the mainstream of English poetry : it has been more typical than not for our great and good poets to show in their later work a hankering after liberties. A poet first learns—or at least this was once the case

—to write in the inherited meters and stanzas, and then—out of adventurous skill or curiosity or ennui—he may seek to loosen and otherwise modify them. He may grow fascinated, as Yeats himself did, by the marriage of high art and ordinary speech; having mastered the tension that results from the various pulls of word, phrase, meter, line, and sentence, he may wonder how far he dare augment that tension, how far he may free the line, without exorcising the ghost. In Yeats's case there is a strong motive from circumstance : it was during his years of intense and varied work with plays—during his first years at the Irish National and Abbey theaters—that he awakened from the insular dream of youth; the beauty and the power of verse (and of heightened prose) designed to be declaimed (or merely delivered, with a strong illusion of naturalness) burned deeply into his sensibility. But it is, as I say, almost a principle that English poets move toward metrical freedom as they mature. No doubt the situation is often reversed today : our young poet inherits metrical inde-terminateness, not stanzas; he emulates not Spenser, Keats, or Landor but Pound, Eliot, or William Carlos Williams. And as that thin or brash or nervous free verse, which reads so much better on the printed page than it delivers, begins to pall, as the Petrarchan sonnet and Wordsworthian nature quatrain have palled, our young poet's adventure may be to move toward orthodoxy. But I am elaborating an aside.

Bridges tells us that, late in life, he had exhausted his own interest in regular meters (he could still delight in Keats and Milton, of course, but when it came to his own work he could not bring himself to use the old line). Although this was not the case with Yeats, the Irish poet, had he been as articulate about prosody as he was about many other matters, would have voiced sentiments at least partly in sympathy with the following observation of the Laureate's :

> It is a natural condition of rhythm, that the common rhythms should be familiar and popular, and they are probably funda-mental, but after familiarity with them the ear soon grows dis-satisfied and wishes them to be broken; it is only those who have no natural ear for rhythm, who can be charmed and contented

with regularity, and they will resent any infraction of it; but those who love rhythm for its own sake know that it is not worth calling rhythm unless it is freely varied, and that rhythm truly begins to be beautiful only when the regularity is broken.[36]

Yeats certainly wanted, as he began to mature, a prosody that would be unusually free to obey the sense and diction. His very passionateness tends to make such a prosody inevitable, and there is also his keen interest in dramatic speech. But of course his embracing of metrical freedom easily follows from the mere increase of realism in an older man. Cadence and irregularity can be maturity's irony replacing (or at least coming alongside and modifying) youth's unseasoned idealism; maturity's solid reflectiveness and ordinary pleasure answering youth's exotic rapture. One can write about "skeleton barks ribbed black against the sunset" only up to "twenty-seven or so"; our attainable felicity, says Melville, is not "in the intellect or the fancy; but in the wife, the heart, the bed, the table, the saddle, the fire-side, the country." Yeats could not write occasional verse, verse with a slice of the times in it, verse on the narrow theater mob or on the struggle over the Lane Gallery, about Crazy Jane or Old Tom, or (without a whine) about his own, his friends', Ireland's, and the modern world's failures, in Pre-Raphaelite rhythms.

Finally, in locating the rationale of Yeats's adherence to meter, one must think about the paradox that meter is. It seems a concomitant of emotion, or at least of heightened vitality. Sun, moon, stars, and the tides beat time; our heart and breath and sometimes our feet are part of the dance; our response to Elgar's great march or to de Lisle's is to march; to the swaying cadences of Beethoven's Sixth Symphony we sway, more intensely alive than we were a moment before. But in some strange way meter is at the same time an embodiment, an ensign, an enactment of inward order and control and normal level of feeling, while the counterpoint of irregularity is what expresses passion, vitality, spontaneity, immediacy. This may be a mystery but it is also a fact. And it is one that is directly relevant to Yeats, on whose birth both Dionysus and Apollo smiled. Yeats does not belie the myth of the passionate Irish heart, though—since he was introverted and almost shy, and since one of his chief passions was for an amicable and courteous atmosphere—he was far from raucous in demeanor. Of course his apotheosis of impulse and passion, of wildness and heedlessness, is in part a mask, the "anti-self" of the quiet literary man, and in part a mocking defiance of the modern prescription that would turn us all into grim realists and brooding existentialists; there is in it, no doubt, even a purely literary echo of Blake. But it is indigenous too. Yeats *is* Irish, and he *is* a poet, and essentially a romantic. He is not nearly as Apollonian a temperament as, say, Bridges or Grey. At the same time, there is a great sanity and charity in Yeats, often overlooked by those who flee his politics and metaphysics. His heart, though it is not a saint's, is right. His political and social counsel was almost always one of moderation and conciliation. His ethic is not relativist or perverse, and the fact that it does not satisfy good modern liberals may be of no great interest to the centuries. He loved and needed detachment but did not reject engagement. For all his mysticism and aestheticism and irrationalism he believed in work, discipline, and responsibility; he transacted business with shrewdness and dispatch; he reported on school conditions; he wrote recommendations on coin design; he went to the senate meetings at a time when public men were being threatened and sometimes shot down.

Meter itself, I am saying, embodies the principle of Yeats's aspiration to "wholeness through oppositions," and in so doing it exercised for him a deep and continual fascination. On the one side, it is an ensign and instrument of emotion, vitality, primitive vigor, engagement in the fury and the mire of human veins; on the other, it is pattern, artifice, aesthetic distance, the golden bird. Yeats is a passionate, thoughtful artist—not merely passionate, thoughtful, or artistic. As with his metrics, he himself has at his best—and he is often at his best—the balance of greatness.

10

The Octaves

Where all's accustomed, ceremonious.
    —Yeats, "A Prayer for My Daughter"

YEATS'S PROSODY has been so little studied that such an obvious innovation as his fondness for octave verse forms in the later work—especially for the surprising *ottava rima*—has gone almost unnoticed. And the fact is that Yeats came into his own at about the time he began taking up the eight-line stanzas. His adoption of them is clearly a striking example of the triumph of a poet's instinct and experience in arriving at a form that allows full expression to the highest powers of his mature genius. During his early years in the theater (around the turn of the century) Yeats woke to the need for a more perceptive and more vigorous style. But a style, an idiom, is not achieved independently of a form. Yeats's transition from minor Irish romanticism to world poetry involved the weaving of a net for golden fish, the discovery of a form that suited him magnificently, that enabled him to make room for all he had to say and all the ways he wanted to say it. The early Yeats is characteristically, as we have seen, a poet of quatrains, the later a poet of octaves. What is most astonishing is his adoption of the *ottava rima*.

By rights Yeats's name ought to be linked forever with the *ottava*, though surprisingly his editors and critics and biographers have been almost silent about his attachment to that famous stanza. He returns to it in his later years again and again. Fifteen of the poems are written wholly or partly in *ottave*.[37] A dozen other poems are pentameter or basically pentameter octaves of various schemes, one of them a stanza which I once thought to be of Yeats's own devising but which Thomas Parkinson has recently pointed out to be Cowley's stanza in the "Ode on the Death of Mr. William Hervey."[38] Another thirty odd poems are nonpentameter octaves. Among these various eight-liners are many of the poems generally held to be among Yeats's most successful; and the general level is very high. The *ottave rime* and the stanzas based on Cowley's Hervey ode are almost unexceptionably admirable; we have here a body of poems that rank sometimes as high as the later odes of Keats (I would put "A Prayer for My Daughter," "Among School Children," and "Sailing to Byzantium" there) and seldom far below them. On the whole, they are inferior to the very best short poems (of comparable scope and form) that have been produced in English only because they are somewhat more private. That is, like much of the rest of Yeats's poetry, they sometimes exhibit a self-absorbed or personally aggressive quality. As a group, though, they are almost entirely free from that histrionic self-dramatization Yeats falls into in his worst moments. The poems I have named immediately above, and (among the octave pieces) a few others, are poetry of negative capability to match Keats's "To Autumn" or Bridges's "Eros." If their coming into being somehow depended on the persisting vitality of pastoralism, theosophy, feudalist politics, and meditation in a lonely tower, then one can only be thankful that our modern emancipation was not sooner or more complete. When I say that the octave poems are as a rule short of the mark of our touchstone poetry by being rather more private, I also mean, of course, that they are sometimes elusive and fuliginous with private symbol and metaphysical system, and private, too, in that readers cannot respond to names like Hazel Lavery or Raftery or Michael Robartes the way Yeats responds—or the way readers themselves respond to Mary or Helen or even, after some effort, to Cuchulain. Still, too much can be made of Yeats's localism; with the precedents of the *Divine Comedy* and Milton's occasional sonnets in mind, we should not dismiss it as mere "disease of romanticism" or of Yeats's own ego. There is enough greatness in the Irish poet that we are left with no defense if we fail to try to justify his persons and places as we do those of Dante.

From 1919 on, Yeats's chief stanzas are octaves and sestets, and the *ottava rima* is one of the favorites.[39] The " Ariosto stanza" seems a peculiar choice for a twentieth-century English poet. We have little tradition of it. Wyatt brought it in, along with the sonnet and *terza rima,* but it failed to arouse much interest (Fulke Greville is about the only poet who keeps coming back to it.) It has remained, in fact, one of the least used of our stanzas (for example, it is one of the few not touched by such prolific poets and eclectic prosodists as Tennyson, Swinburne, and Bridges; and the master Milton, too, with all his knowledge and love of things Italian, left us with that single miraculous envoi at the close of *Lycidas*). In 1927, when "Sailing to Byzantium" (composed in the autumn of 1926) was published, the only *ottava* poem still circulating with any vitality among English readers was Byron's *Don Juan.* A reader will search Yeats's prose and letters in vain for any mention of the *ottave* as such; and, to my knowledge, no one has yet ventured an opinion as to his model. He may well have learned the tune from Byron or from Shelley (a poet he liked rather better); the latter used the stanza after 1820 for a number of poems (and interesting fragments) which are little known but which, in their unusual tension of dignified lyric feeling and easy, informal meditativeness, are tonally much closer to Yeats than anything in *Don Juan* or Byron's other *ottave.* Yeats published a little poem—it is not good and not

extremely bad, but the poet chose not to include it in the
Collected Poems—titled "A Dawn Song" in *The Irish Fireside*
of February 5, 1887. It is four stanzas of trochaic tetrameter in
ottava rima scheme—a rare, perhaps a unique, form and
certainly the only one of its kind in Yeats's entire work. Nearly
four decades lie between it and the first of the true *ottave* :
surely the latter do not germinate from some memory or recon-
sideration of this distant and innocuous little piece. And yet
its existence does make one hesitate to assume with absolute
confidence that Yeats never caught sight of *ottava rima* until
his advanced maturity. It seems to me unlikely that he would
have written an odd, almost parodic, variant on *ottava rima*
without having known—known in the sense of really having
considered the form—the true Ariostan. And Yeats had been
reading Shelley admiringly in the late 1880's. But I offer this
connection with Shelley only as a passing speculation. All sorts
of hypotheses are possible. The facts, it seems, are lost to us.
Fortunately it is more important to try to make sense of
Yeats's choice of the *ottava* in terms of his aims and previous
practice than to worry about possible models.

It is good to guard against assuming that because of a
certain prosodic logic the transition from a four-line to an
eight-line unit was an easy thing for Yeats to manage. It is by
no means a certainty that a poet will be able to master the
very verse form closest to the one he has already perfected;
the *ottava rima*, in particular, is both a double quatrain and
something different. Had Yeats not been able to make the
necessary adjustment, he would still be an important poet;
but it is only necessary to go through the *Collected Poems,*
deleting all the octave pieces, to see what would have been
lost. And that, of course, is an oversimplified test : oftentimes
it is the writing of a good poem in one sort of metrics that
allows a poet to write another poem in a different sort, and
Yeats's poems are notoriously interdependent, lending one
another reciprocal energy and meaning in ever more intricate
congeries as the body of poems accumulates (this is of course
in some ways unfortunate, since even the most superior readers
are usually desultory readers; it does give Yeats solidity and

continuity). For Yeats the poems in regular forms seem to have been necessary if there were to be any poems of a less regular character; his mind, as we have seen, was distinctly of the type that works in form and then sometimes and to some extent away from it. When he grew tired of the form, or felt confined by it, he could roll up his sleeves and shatter it— ever so masterfully, the mastery having been developed in working for so long within the strict bounds.

But if the octaves in general are to be seen as a natural step for Yeats to take in elaborating a larger complex of thought and feeling than he found easily workable in quatrain, the choice of the *ottava rima* reflects originality as well as conservatism or continuity. In fact, it must have delighted Yeats, for besides being roomy, allowing a pithy couplet when needed, and offering in its repeated rhymes the possibility of an incantatory effect, it reconciled contraries. It was both highly traditional (in Italian poetry and vicariously in English) and yet—as Yeats wanted to develop it, as a texture of the compact and the symbolic at home with the conversational— little tried by English poets. Even the difficulty of the *ottava* probably attracted Yeats, who rather enjoyed difficulties, for the sake of the stimulation and for the strength gained in the contest. Yeats was an aesthete, but not a hedonist, and not even a ripe papaya aesthete. His manner was gracious and rather deferent; he was a listener; unlike his idol Landor he was conciliatory and would rather lose an argument than a friend. He said truly of himself that he was a timid man except on paper; but there are degrees of timidity, too, and Yeats was no tergiversator. He was responsible in life as in art, and had a northern capacity for work, discipline, and contest. One thinks of the stress he knew in his work at the theaters and of his argument for divorce in the address before the Irish senate, of his constant defense of pastoral, conservative, and mentalist ways and biases in a century whose hero was increasingly urban, liberal, and materialist.

It was undoubtedly the combination of Yeats's stubbornness and special genius for a quatrain that enabled him to see his way through to the *ottava*. That it is a refractory stanza for an English poet (for serious poetry) is well known. Its infrequent appearance in English and its infrequent success when it does appear would be enough to confirm its difficulty; and it may be revealing that most of the poets who have done anything at all with the stanza have taken it up only late in their craft. One of Spenser's two *ottava* poems, "Muiopotmos," was written in advanced maturity; the other, "Virgil's Gnat," is earlier and much inferior. Shelley did not use the stanza until after 1820; Byron adopted it only toward the end of his career; Browning, I believe, used it for a single poem ("Pan and Luna") and that a late one. All this may of course be coincidence : elaborate verse forms have as often as not appealed to ambitious young English poets. But our limited rhyme vocabulary does militate against the two triple rhymes needed in the *ottava*, and the repetitive rhyme itself can produce a certain monotony; the concluding couplet tends, as in the Shakespearean sonnet, to isolate itself, at some risk of disunity. Byron's counter to the monotony was a racy, random style; and his eclectic wit and spice allowed a range of rhymes not available for a more serious idiom. Yeats countered both monotony and scarcity of rhyme by liberal use of slant rhyme as well as by working hard for perfectly functional rhyme words.

But much as the difficulty of the *ottava* might have attracted rather than discouraged Yeats, and right as its historical associations may have seemed to him, obviously these would have been minor considerations. It was, I believe, mainly the room of the octave that he was after : a larger stanza to carry the scope and penetration of a mature spirit. The same principle, though it makes for no romantic or ingenious explanation, would account for the great increase in sestets (as compared) with the earlier dominance of quatrains) that one sees in the later work. And as I have already pointed out, the Ariostan octave in particular readily lends itself to certain predilections of the seasoned Yeats : it invites resonance and incantation, and makes available the synoptic or epigrammatic couplet.

Yeats's previous mastery of quatrains cannot but have

stood him in good stead when he started to take up octave forms; they would have helped him even with the *ottava,* which, in his as in Italian practice, frequently has the structure of a double quatrain. This 4–4 structure of the stanza is equally evident in the early, popular Sicilian *ottava* songs and in the verse of Boccaccio, Ariosto, and Poliziano. Here, for example, are two stanzas taken quite at random (the first is from Poliziano's *La Giostra,* the second from *Orlando Furioso*); notice the division into distinct quatrains :

> *Ell' era assisa sopra la verdura*
> *Allegra, e ghirlandetta avea contesta*
> *Di quanti fior creasse mai natura,*
> *De 'quali era dipinta la sua vesta.*
> *E come prima al giovan pose cura,*
> *Alquanto paurosa also latesta:*
> *Poi con la bianca man ripreso il lembo,*
> *Levossi in pie con di fior pieno un grembo.*
>
> I.47)

> (Reclined she was upon a grassy mound,
> With every flower that ever nature made
> She wove a garland that she might be crowned,
> And with those flowers her vesture was arrayed.
> When first she saw the youth she turned her round,
> Seeing that youth her eyes grew half afraid,
> Then, raising the border of her gown, she rose,
> Her lap, a garden filled with every flower that grows.)
>
> (tr. Iain Fletcher)

> *Credi che Dio questi ignoranti ha privi*
> *De lo 'ntelleto, e loro offusca i lumi;*
> *Che de la poesia gli ha fatto schivi,*
> *Accio che morte il tutto ne consumi.*
> *Oltre che del sepolcro uscirian vivi,*
> *Ancor ch'avesser tutti i rei costumi,*
> *Pur che sapesson farsi amica Cirra,*
> *Piu grato odore avrian che nardo o mirra.*
>
> (XXXV.24)

> (Believe me, these fools are in God's hands!
> Such senseless absence of enlightenment,

Shunning poet and poetry, unwittingly plans
Oblivion for them, unbroken, after death.
And yet, they might make shrouds mere swaddling-bands,
Though in their lives the guiltiest and worst men,
If they befriended some Parnassian singer:
Then, they might still smell sweet as nard or myrrh!)
                                    (tr. Edwin Morgan)

In these examples the couplet simply continues the lyricism
and particularity of the preceding six lines; it is in each case
an integral part of the second quatrain. Just as frequently, of
course, it serves that purpose for which it is so aptly suited :
the sapient comment or conclusion. It is used in that way, for
example, in the first two stanzas of "Sailing to Byzantium,"
the first-written and still the best-known of Yeats's *ottave*.
The first six lines of the Byzantium poem image, in a depre-
catory but not disgusted or uncharitable tone, both the world
that belongs to the dynamic, sense-preoccupied young and the
world in general—the whole temporal sphere of birth, growth,
breeding, death. What "that country" brings forth is, however
vital and engaging for a while, soon to die and soon to be
outgrown. When one is not yet old, it is possible to be a vibrat-
ing part of that "sensual music"; but what is a scarecrow to
do among a company of the young in one another's arms?
Suddenly the stanza turns; the elaboration of the image is
over, there is a full stop, and the couplet rejects the picture
aphoristically :

> Caught in that sensual music all neglect
> Monuments of unageing intellect.

In the poem's second stanza the function of the couplet is
somewhat the same; here it is an emphatic report of action
taken, following an explanation of what the aged poet's decision should be.

Neither of the poem's first two stanzas, then, shows a division into two distinct quatrains. Such division does occur,
however, and not infrequently. We see it, for example, in the
two final stanzas of "Among School Children"; it will be well
to give them here in their entirety :

VII

Both nuns and mothers worship images,
But those the candles light are not as those
That animate a mother's reveries,
But keep a marble or a bronze repose.
And yet they too break hearts—O Presences
That passion, piety or affection knows,
And that all heavenly glory symbolize—
O self-born mockers of man's enterprise;

VIII

Labour is blossoming or dancing where
The body is not bruised to pleasure soul,
Nor beauty born out of its own despair,
Nor blear-eyed wisdom out of midnight oil.
O chestnut-tree, great-rooted blossomer,
Are you the leaf, the blossom, or the bole?
O body swayed to music, O brightening glance,
How can we know the dancer from the dance?

At the end of the fourth line of stanza VII there is a significant, though not complete, transition in the line of argument;
at the close of the stanza there is another transition, but this
time so slight a one that the thought must run on into the next
stanza. In this final stanza the argument is completed at the
end of the fourth line, and the remaining four lines form an
ecstatic apostrophe, the great change in intensity and approach
necessitating a quatrain fully cut off grammatically from the
preceding lines. Because the argument carries over between
stanzas and because the final stanza culminates in a glorious
rhetorical question, there is no call for aphoristic, set-off
couplets.

Yeats's other principal eight-line stanza is not the brace or
the "heroic" octaves but the unusual stanza of "A Prayer for
My Daughter," "Byzantium," and other poems. Yeats usually
adopts it in preference to the *ottava* whenever a poem is more
purely lyrical or lyrically descriptive, and somewhat less philo-

sophic, or whenever there are to be relatively sharp contrasts of tone—contrasts the versification helps vivify by varying lengths of line and changes in meter.

Thus "Colonus' Praise" is largely a poem of lyric mythological description, full of wonder on glories past. "Byzantium" is, in a way, a sequel to the earlier Byzantium poem. It is the seeing of a vision; the earlier poem is decision and desire and supplication—all enriched by an undertone of faint, mellow humor (an undertone often missed by the poem's explicators). "Byzantium" is phantasmagoria, the earlier poem is generalized and philosophical; the former is incantatory, the latter not. "Byzantium" is descriptive and in a fairly particular way; the city itself suggests more strongly than is the case in the earlier poem the historical medieval Byzantium. There is the Eastern imagery of the emperor's soldiery, the dome, the cathedral gong. The "Prayer for My Daughter," now anxiously, now worshipfully and placidly lyrical, modulates through a number of keys and utilizes wonderfully the effect of opening or expansiveness for which this particular stanza is well suited. "In Memory of Major Robert Gregory" and the second part of "The Tower" are poetry of highly specific personal reminiscence. So, of course, is the regular *ottava* poem "The Municipal Gallery Revisited," but the latter has a dignity and retrospective complexity of thought and imagery compatible with the more formal, or perhaps I should say homogeneous, stanza.

And so this rare and unusually constructed octave is in Yeats's handling another perfect match of outward form and informing spirit. It uses couplets with an intention entirely different from the *sententiae* of the *ottava* : the form opens out all the way instead of tending to accumulate its energy toward an emphatic and often synoptic close :

> May she become a flourishing hidden tree
> That all her thoughts may like the linnet be,
> And have no business but dispensing round
> Their magnanimities of sound,
> Nor but in merriment begin a chase,

> Nor but in merriment a quarrel.
> O may she live like some green laurel
> Rooted in one dear perpetual place.

The whole scheme expands and lightens, going away from the couplet rather than toward it, and away from the fullness of the pentameter. The closing rhyme (*c*) is separated from its mate by the *d* brace, the distance rendering an effect of expansion and freedom. The fourth, sixth, and seventh lines are typically tetrameter (in "Byzantium" some of them are trimeters, and there is even a dimeter), providing a lyric relief from the full breath of the decasyllabics. Almost invariably the couplets themselves are open, not closed, and they rarely stand out as relatively isolated units of sententiousness; frequently they are purely descriptive and mood-setting, as in the opening stanzas of the prayer:

> Once more the storm is howling, and half hid
> Under this cradle-hood and coverlid
> My child sleeps on. There is no obstacle
> But Gregory's wood and one bare hill
>
> I have walked and prayed for this young child an hour
> And heard the sea-winds scream upon the tower,
> And under the arches of the bridge, and scream
> In the elms above the flooded stream. . . .

This most songlike of the Yeats octaves becomes a yet more distinctly lyrical stanza—is made the more amenable to sharper contrasts and more intense effects generally—by the variation of meter Yeats permits in the short lines. In them he not infrequently substitutes trochaic meter or speech cadence for the expected iambic, as in the tetrameter couplet of the second stanza of this same poem:

> That the future years had come,
> Dancing to a frenzied drum . . . .

Here the trochaic measure—through its inherent strength or prominence and its contrast with the surrounding iambic—helps convey the father's anxiety and imaginative susceptibility, which at this point in the poem have reached a shrill peak.

It would be foolish to insist that one can trace a hard and fast distinction between the kind of poem for which Yeats uses the *ottava rima* and the kind for which he uses the Cowleian octave, but the general distinction, as I have tried to sketch it here, seems to hold. The right instinct that led Yeats on from the quatrain to the greater space and greater aphoristic and incantatory potential of the *ottava* continued, in that it suggested something different from the *ottava* and other homogeneous octaves for certain qualities of feeling.

The natural growth from quatrain to octave and sestet is in itself cogent evidence of the organic character of Yeats's development and of the conservative cast of his mind. Here is no Poe, Rimbaud, or Hart Crane but a poet with inward composure and a reserve of strength that could control and direct the irrational element in his nature and meet experience responsibly and manfully. It would seem that he took up octave stanzas because he needed a larger stanza or two to go alongside (not replace) his quatrains; the same holds true for the sestets he came to favor during the same period. They meant a moderate, rather than a sharp, change for him, and his years of practice in quatrains had prepared him for larger stanzas with an even number of lines. The *ottava rima* particularly attracted him : it allowed ample working room; it was a challenge; it was both traditional and little used; it provided a reflective couplet for his increasing aphoristic bent and power; and like the Cowleian octave, it allowed resonant and incantatory effects.

It is not putting the case too strongly, I believe, to say that it was as much Yeats's achievement of the octaves as his development of a rich and flexible new idiom that allowed him the full fruition of his powers.

11

The Verse of the Plays

In poetic drama the broken, few rhythms of our daily
speech are implemented and supplemented until they
have an enlarged life. . . . To show us the things
that man would say if he could; to show us—like
something at the heart of a crystal—the thoughts that
are governing his life, and that the lesser tensions
of daily speech will not permit him to utter.

—Gordon Bottomley

IT IS CHIEFLY by his short poems that Yeats lives and will continue to live. Yet he wrote plays at the beginning of his career and continued to write them until the very end. *The Countess Cathleen* belongs to 1892, *Purgatory* and *The Death of Cuchulain* to 1939; between them come nearly two dozen more plays (the figure becomes nearly three dozen if one includes the "unauthorized" versions and the uncollected or unpublished dramatic juvenilia). Estimates of Yeats's success as a playwright vary. Most of the pieces read better than they play. In this respect Yeats is well above Robert Bridges and almost on a par with Synge. Wide appeal (outside Ireland)

and stageworthiness at any price were never among his aims. His plays are experiments, and not in neat plotting or naturalistic realization of character. Generally they are too lyrical to be dramatic and too condensed to satisfy our hunger for an action "of some magnitude." Some of them are strangely hybrid, as close to ballet or pantomime as to the play proper, more phantasmagoria than plot. Their predilection is to sacrifice the traditional essentials of drama—plot and character —for a gain in sensitive beauty (spiritual and linguistic) and in passionateness; likewise, the ideal of immediate clarity of language is not infrequently sacrificed for freshness and richness. At their best, as in *The Countess Cathleen, Deirdre,* and *On Baile's Strand,* they strike a happy medium between that which will hold an ordinary variegated audience and that which will hold an audience of scholars, critics, painters, poets, dancers, and musicians; but the balance is always tipped at least slightly toward the latter group. Audiences the least homogeneous have found beauty and power in several of these plays. Their spiritual and poetic—and sometimes even their dramatic—superiority to most of the plays one encounters today in the experimental or "little" theater, and in fact to most of the plays of Yeats's successors, cannot be questioned. But whatever one's opinions, one must take the plays into account. They pose—the later ones particularly—many problems and have occasioned many arguments, not only in regard to merit but to interpretation itself. In the present book I am concerned solely with the verse of the plays, a subject which, especially when one arrives at *Purgatory* and *The Herne's Egg,* offers sufficient difficulty of its own. I will not enter into interpretive and evaluative discussion where it does not directly illuminate Yeats's choice and handling of the medium. The Irish poet's beliefs and attitudes and interests are unmistakably revealed in the content of the plays. Like the poems they show us at once a sensitive, nervously energetic, deeply responsive, rather "literary," visionary man of catholic interests, a man who is a romantic traditionalist and also a modern in his doubt, his will to believe, his fascination with myth and history, his love of realistic and colloquial language, and of course in many other things. In the plays, as in the poems and elsewhere, the key words are beauty, nobility, religion, passion, song, imagination. One sees Yeats's aristocratic temper not only in theme and sentiment but in his very decision to forego the mass audience and write for the elect (or at any rate for the few who in his opinion would constitute an elect). All this is right on the surface, and no one can miss or mistake it. My present concern is with the forms into which Yeats shapes the language of his plays : forms over which he exercises control and through which are inevitably revealed habits of mind and patterns of development.

It will be best to begin by grouping the plays, in a general way, according to their time of composition and their use of prose and verse.

Nine of the plays in the authorized collection are in prose. The other seventeen are in verse of one sort or another. All of the prose plays contain verse as well, either in the form of songs or in short passages of verse dialogue, or both. Several of the verse plays, likewise, contain stretches of prose dialogue. In every case, however, the plays are basically the one or the other. All but three of the earlier plays (*Cathleen Ni Houlihan, The Pot of Broth,* and *The Unicorn from the Stars*) are verse. The 1922 *Player Queen* is prose and is followed by five more prose plays. The next two (*A Full Moon in March* and *The King of the Great Clock Tower,* both 1935) are verse plays that are fairly regular in their blank verse and full of rhyme. Two of the final three plays are verse of an experimental and proselike sort. *The Death of Cuchulain,* the last play, is (after an introductory passage of prose) blank verse, but blank verse the loosest, the most irregular, Yeats wrote :

> Scullions, armourers, bed-makers and messengers,
> Until they hammer me with a ladle, cut me with a knife . . .

> Somebody said that I was in Maeve's tent,
> And somebody else, a big man by his voice,
> That if I brought Cuchulain's head in a bag
> I would be given twelve pennies; I had the bag. . . .

That is the general picture. It is complicated slightly by

the fact that Yeats was constantly revising the plays—often radically—and by the fact that a number of the plays exist in both verse and prose versions. *The Green Helmet* is a verse rendition of a suppressed prose play titled *The Golden Helmet*; *The Hour-Glass,* a verse play in 1913, had been written as prose a decade earlier; *A Full Moon in March* and *The King of the Great Clock Tower,* now verse plays, were first drafted in prose; *Fighting the Waves* is a prose version of *The Only Jealousy of Emer.* Nor do we know all the details of Yeats's composition : some of the manuscripts, particularly among the earlier work, have not survived; and the account that may be pieced together from Yeats's own commentaries and correspondence and from the surviving commentary of those who knew him is by no means complete. Nevertheless, out of all this history a direction becomes distinctly visible—though, as usual, Yeats prefers to travel in crooked ways rather than in a straight one. The general story is this. He moves away from regular and orthodox metrical form (after having mastered it) and toward the freedom and realism of looser rhythms and of prose itself. The whole pattern runs absolutely parallel with the body of the poems : from the regular to the irregular; from the quality of statuary to the quality of realism in word and rhythm within a still poetic and romantic or symbolist context; from sweet melancholy to irony and intellectual sinewiness. But it is not, I say, a straight line; and there is no reason why it should be. In the midst of this loosening of metric comes the old iambic regularity of *A Full Moon in March* and *The King of the Great Clock Tower.* The experimental verse of two of the last plays—*The Herne's Egg* and *Purgatory*—makes one think, too, that Yeats took up prose not only to suit his growing realism (which is never, of course, "the realism of the machine shop") but also as the result of a search for a flexible medium that would be more adaptable than blank verse, more adaptable to the whole range of effects he was striving for. He had tried prose before; now he would try it again, this time a more discursive, more conventional, no longer folk-poetic prose. Compare, for example, the two passages below. The first is from *Cathleen Ni Houlihan* (1902), the second from *The Resurrection* (1931):

> *Old Woman.* Sometimes my feet are tired and my hands are quiet, but there is no quiet in my heart. When the people see me quiet, they think old age has come on me and that all the stir has gone out of me. But when the trouble is on me I must be talking to my friends.

> *The Greek.* What seems their indifference is but their eternal possession of themselves. Man, too, remains separate. He does not surrender his soul. He keeps his privacy.

Of course the sensible man of the theater will step in here and tell us that Yeats's progressive favoring of prose or very loose metric for the later plays may well be explained by a most pedestrian fact: the poet may have begun to despair of verse for the quite simple reason that—as he himself exclaims in the 1934 Preface to the *Collected Plays*—"speakers of verse are rare." I think we should be ready to admit that there is a point here; yet though despair of finding adequate deliverers of verse may have influenced Yeats to give more and more opportunity to the "other harmony," this chagrin was almost certainly not the main spur. The whole body of poems has shown us that Yeats became progressively more enchanted by a prosody which has broken away from strict regularity, and especially by the artful suggestion of speech cadence within a still metrical frame. Besides, his aims and his character, as we have seen, were such as to cause him to prefer, on the whole, song and verse dialogue inadequately delivered to Shavian repartee or Ibsenesque laconism expertly articulated. That he was in fact much disturbed by the difficulties of rendering verse effectively from the stage and that he decided nevertheless to stick with the ship, is so obvious from the least acquaintance with his essays, letters, and notes on the plays as to require no documentation. It is perhaps supererogatory to point out that his last play is a thing of rhyme and meter and that two of the late verse plays—*A Full Moon in March* and *The King of the Great Clock Tower*—were originally prose pieces.

The verse of *The Herne's Egg* and of *Purgatory*—which has received an accolade from T. S. Eliot—is (like the plays themselves) a perplexing matter. A close look at it is in order.

What we have here, it seems to me, is a compromise between prose and verse. The lines are to be scanned, I believe, as accentual verse—verse whose principle is that each line contains the same number of primary stresses but an indeterminate number of weaker stresses (or "nonstresses"). But Yeats's handling of the measure is very irregular; the rhythm is loose enough to give the effect of heightened prose. Typically the verse of these two plays shows three or four strong stresses to a line :

> *Congal.* Tara and I have made a peace;
>
> Our fiftieth battle fought, there is need
>
> Of preparation for the next;
>
> He and all his principal men,
>
> I and all my principal men.
>
> Take supper at his principal house
>
> This night, in his principal city, Tara.
> . . . .
>
> Those leaps may carry her where
>
> No woman has gone, and he
>
> Extinguish sun, moon, star.
>
> No bridal torch can burn
>
> When his black midnight is there.
>   —*The Herne's Egg,* Scene II

But it will rise to as high as five stresses, as in lines five and seven of the first passage above, or as in this line :

> To fool us all; but Great Herne or another

and it will drop to as low as two, as in the third line of the first passage above, or as in these lines:

> Though that be terrible . . .
>
> She is but a puppet. . . .

The lines are most often of eight syllables (as in the first of the longer passages above, in which four of the seven lines are octosyllabic). But they may contain as few as five:

> No, never again . . .

or as many as twelve:

> Show it to the people and get all the pennies . . .

or even fifteen, as in the last line of *Purgatory*:

> The misery of the living and the remorse of the dead.

The rhythmic effect of both plays is neither that of prose nor of blank verse. It is more regular and more stylized than ordinary prose cadence and generally less so than unrhymed pentameter. The feeling that one is hearing verse—to the extent that one does feel so—is created not only by the relative regularity in the number of beats to a line but also by the sense of line which Yeats maintains by such means as completing a major phase of syntax at the end of the line, terminal caesura, stichomythia, and parallelism of words and phrases and syntactic structures between lines. All of these line-marking devices are combined, of course, in stichomythia. Notice that in the example below, from the second scene of *The Herne's Egg,* the effect is particularly emphatic because the lines themselves are so short:

> *Mary.* Have all those fierce men gone?
> *Attracta.* All those fierce men have gone.
> *Agnes.* But they will come again?
> *Attracta.* No, never again.
> *Kate.* We bring three presents.
> *Mary.* This is a jug of cream.
> *Agnes.* This is a bowl of butter.
> *Kate.* This is a basket of eggs.

I do not put this forth as fine poetry or even as effective stage dialogue (my own opinion of *The Herne's Egg* is that it is histrionic rather than dramatic, and obscure even to most of the "audience of fifty or a hundred" Yeats was writing for). I say that such a passage does create the effect of verse and is very emphatic.

One begins to see that the verse form of these two plays is not as radical a departure from tradition or from Yeats's own previous practice as it may appear at first encounter. In fact it continues to reflect two principles we have discerned all along in Yeats's character: his love of tradition and order and the continuity of his development—the growth of the tree, not the change of the chameleon; the evolution of the conservative, not the fits and starts of the neoterist. The verse measure of these plays is in harmony with tradition first of all because it does remain a kind of verse, an ordering beyond the order needed to secure syntactical clarity, proper rhetorical emphasis, and some degree of harmony; and secondly because three-beat and four-beat accentual verse has been very common in English poetry from the time of *Beowulf*. The measure seems to me an organic extension of two of Yeats's favorite forms: rhyming septasyllabic and octosyllabic verse. I do not wish to appear ingenious or to scan this verse at any cost. But we have here a peculiar coincidence if we do not have a case in which those old and mastered forms are stripped of their rhyme and very much loosened.

As with his poems, so with his plays: Yeats moves from tradition to experiment (in language and in dramatic technique, of course, as well as in metric, and from strict and rather traditional to less regular and more personal forms). But there is nothing dogmatic about this movement, and Yeats leaves open behind him all the old paths. He is a literary artist not content merely to repeat his successes or, in any event, his manner; a man who, for all his love of tradition, possesses also a quick and even somewhat restless, rather than a lethargic, temperament; a perfectionist, whose search for better—or at least for different and equally suitable—forms is, after all, one aspect of an ambition of which his notorious continual re-

vision is another. Further, the odd medium of *The Herne's
Egg* and *Purgatory*—half verse, half prose, but both together,
and not exactly "prose poetry" either—suggests Yeats's search
for the reconciliation of opposites :

> Study that tree.
> It stands there like a purified soul,
> All cold, sweet, glistening light.
> Dear mother, the window is dark again,
> But you are in the light because
> I finished all that consequence.

However unsuited such lines may be to drama as stage fare—
an art that never dare be obscure—they possess in their own
right the simplicity, directness, and irregular rhythms of prose
and speech and the intensity and indirection of poetry. It is
the same fusion of prose and poetic qualities that Yeats sought
in many of the short poems of his maturity.

Yeats was a great synthesizer, and perhaps we are to
understand the verse of these late plays as another instance of
the attempt he was making in his late poems to draw together
into an equipoise the virtues of poetry, prose, and speech, that
is, to achieve a carry-all form, a form capable of the most
diverse themes and effects; he would create a medium for the
stage as protean as his octaves. Blank verse is a wonderfully
adaptable instrument; but after one loosens it beyond a certain point it tends to become flaccid and to smack not so much
of the irregularity of actual speech as of the incompetence of
the playwright to compose speech that anyone would want
to hear. Yeats seems to me to be asking whether there is not
some worthy successor to unrhymed pentameter, some other
instrument that could sound with the compelling accent of
current speech the note of passion or the note of gentle irony,
that could sound in one chord the tone that vibrates from a
mind at once worldly wise and instinctively committed to
transcendent values, that could move freely and without strain
from rough satire or frank sexuality to tender appreciation,
from highly personal reminiscence to impersonal epigram.

In the plays, too, as in the poems, Yeats refuses *vers libre*.

Here again the situation is no doubt complicated. Partly it is that love of bringing opposites into equilibrium which causes him to reject this mode that proved so very attractive to so many of the better poets during Yeats's mature years. Partly, too, the adherence to a norm of at least a rough accentualism in the freest of his plays, as to a norm of rhyme or meter in the freest of his later poems, is another demonstration of his love of order—indeed, of his passion for it. The man who could write of aristocracy in an almost devotional tone, who could find something to admire in every hierarchic system, and who kept order in his family, his business, and his public obligations, could be expected to hold onto some formal principle in every piece of poetry.

I would say, too, that yet another impulse is to be discerned in Yeats's desire to maintain in the midst of freedom the effect of verse : the impulse to chant. To render the effect of incantation, poetry must look to repetition and parallelism —in rhythmic unit as in word, image, and syntax. Incantation expresses and is meant to evoke strong feeling, and here lies, I think, still another reason for Yeats's innovating the accentual verse of these two plays. His search for a prosodic carry-all was also perhaps a search for a medium that would declaim better than the verse of the early plays. Marlowe early showed us that blank verse can be made to declaim; but Yeats does not seem to be able to make it do so with any great success, perhaps because he had succeeded so well in making it on the one hand conversational and on the other visionary and marmoreal. Also he may well have seen that for the strident, exclamatory feelings he often cultivated as he grew older, he would do well to abandon the traditional verse altogether (at times) and look for a mode that, for him at least, could be made rather consistently ejaculatory. Certainly the lovely measure of *Deirdre* and *The Countess Cathleen* would not do for the disjointed, percussive quality of *The Herne's Egg* or for the tense, unhappy phantasmagoria of *Purgatory*. I would not press this conjecture, but it does seem to me that Yeats's blank verse is very often unsuccessful when it attempts to express violent passion. With Yeats unrhymed pentameter seems to have its provenance in softness and sweetness, in melancholy and praise and reflectiveness; seeking declamatory power, it becomes grandiloquent or even prosaic. The sweet sensuousness of

> You're fair to look upon.
> Your feet delight in dancing, and your mouths
> In the slow smiling that awakens love.
> The mothers that have borne you mated rightly.
> They'd little ears as thirsty as your ears
> For many love songs . . .
> —*The King's Threshold* (1904)

is greatly superior to the exultant

> O silver trumpets, be you lifted up
> And cry to the great race that is to come.
> Long-throated swans upon the waves of time,
> Sing loudly, for beyond the wall of the world
> That race may hear our music and awake.
> —ibid.

I have pointed out that even in his early poetry Yeats shows a certain desire to experiment metrically, especially to loosen or relax his meter. The blank verse of the early plays shows the same tendency. It is another indication of how the plays and poems go hand in hand, of the consistency of Yeats's instinct for metric.

Notice the irregularity—in both count of syllables and actual positions of stresses—of the passage below, which is found in the first part of *The King's Threshold* :

> *Seanchan.*   He has great strength
> And great patience to hold his right hand there,
> Uplifted, and not wavering about.
> He is much stronger than I am, much stronger.

The second line is highly irregular—"patience" does not make an iamb, and sense demands that "hand" receive stress, although both "right" and "there" are already stressed by position. In the uniambic and simply unmetrical eleven syllables of "He is much stronger than I am, much stronger," the cadence of ordinary speech takes over. Here is another passage from the same play :

> *Second Cripple.* Have pity on us, that must beg our bread
> From table to table throughout the entire world. . . .

The second line there shows twelve syllables and no iambic rhythm at all.

One more instance will suffice. The passage below makes up the second speech of the First Musician in the opening of *Deirdre* (1907):

> 1 Some dozen years ago, King Concubar found*
> 2 A house upon a hillside in this wood,
> 3 And there a child with an old witch to nurse her,
> 4 And nobody to say if she were human,
> 5 Or of the gods, or anything at all
> 6 Of who she was or why|she was hid|den there,
> 7 But that she'd too much beauty for good luck.
> 8 He went up thither daily, till at last
> 9 She put on womanhood, and he lost peace,
> 10 And Deirdre's tale began. The King was old.
> 11 A month or so before the marriage-day,
> 12 A young man, in the laughing scorn|of his youth,
> 13 Naoise, the son of Usna, climbed up there,*
> 14 And having wooed, or, as some say, been wooed,
> 15 Carried her off.

The diction and syntax are ordinary speech; there are no syntactical inversions or other oddities. The iambic basis makes itself felt but is greatly relaxed; every line shows at least one point of variation from the theoretical pattern, and most of the lines show two or three deviations; the word or phrase that makes up the iambic foot is usually tied syllabi- cally or phrasally right into a following syllable or word— diaeresis is avoided. Notice, too, Yeats's characteristic use of the anapestic substitution (I have marked it in lines 6 and 12).

*Yeats's pronunciations : kon o har, ne she.

This irregularizing of meter prefigures the cadenced metric of *The Herne's Egg* and *Purgatory* and the very loose iambics of some of the later plays.

Finally, one notices the persistence of rhyme in the plays as in the poems. From Aleel's first song in *The Countess Cathleen*—"Were I but crazy for love's sake"—it goes right on; the free measures of the last plays are well larded with it. *The Green Helmet* is rhymed throughout. But I can say nothing about the significance of this devotion to rhyme without repeating what I have said in Chapter 8 or anticipating my summary remarks in the next chapter.

12

The Cards on the Table

. . . In prosody all the cards are laid on the table.
—Karl Shapiro

FROM this study of the metrical shapes Yeats gave to his poetry over a period of half a century, we have seen that he worked relentlessly at his art of verse, devoting himself to obtaining maximum control of his timbres, rhythms, and verse forms. Concurrent with this discipline was an apparently instinctive sense of appropriate form. In any case, we have seen that his "bitter hours" (spent in shaping a poem) were again and again blessed with success.

We have also noticed that his art shows a remarkable continuity reconciled with no small degree of change and development. The prosodic ties between the earlier and the later poems are stronger than random reading of the poems or an acquaintance with the critical canon would suggest. Because the critics (with very few exceptions) have dealt impressionistically or not at all with Yeats's metrics, and because they have often emphasized the obvious and sometimes striking contrasts (as in diction and attitude) between the youthful and the mature art, they have generally failed to see how strong the parallels are.

One notices the unbroken adherence to rhyme (in some form) and the tendency of the earlier poetry toward relatively great license in rhyme, a license that soon becomes an active interest in slant rhyme. The greater metrical freedom of the later poems and plays is foreshadowed in the considerable metrical variety and freedom one finds in some of the early ones. The sestets and the *ottave rime* and other octaves are not a sudden innovation of Yeats's mature years, but a development from the early quatrains. And the quatrains themselves persist strongly to the end. Yeats managed to continue —after, one must add, reviving it from its Decadent enfeeblement—the great, indigenous quatrain tradition of English poetry; and of course the many sestet and octave stanzas of his later years, in which so much of his best work is cast, are an extension of that tradition. What is revealed in such splendid recovery and extension is, besides great mental vigor and capacity for discipline, an inner stability and confidence and a bold yet strongly conservative temperament. Yeats's traditionalism is not mere rational conviction; it is certainly not pose—though, like any attitude, it might be, if occasion demanded, posed in the sense of being thrust belligerently forward in mocking exaggeration or in defiance of modern neoterism and sciolism, of shallow "liberalism" and democratic vulgarity and mediocrity. The prosody is in some way the man, and it reveals, as the words that make up the prosody reveal, a man who in his thought and affections alike was never a democrat.

We see Yeats also as the type of poet who imposes his will upon the verse rather than the type who sets himself a form to fill and then listens to its heuristic suggestions in order to spur and supplement a thin or lethargic imagination. Of course, every poem has to get written, and no matter how much the poet brings "ready" to the time of composition, he will invariably at some point in his progress toward the final caesura find himself begging and hopeful, soliciting from the form to which he is working and from the material he has already spun out, an image, a transitional tonality, an extension or qualification of his conception at this point and at that. No poem—at least, no verse, no poem that uses any sort of prosodic pattern—is wholly the result of an initial determination to say certain things, and certain things only, in an absolutely preconceived tone and structure. To some degree every poet must always submit himself to the words he has set down at the moment and to the adopted or envisioned verse form, letting word lead to word, one line to another, a rhyme to an idea, and an idea to another rhyme. And once he has decided upon a particular verse form—Italian sonnet, say, or stave of six—he has to put up with the choices permitted or demanded by that particular form. But Yeats, unlike a poet such as Dobson or Swinburne, has, to start things moving, such rich and deeply felt congeries of thought and feeling and observation that most of the time the easier forms and the forms he has already learned and made habitual will do perfectly well to articulate the developing vision. He does not have the disadvantage, as Robert Bridges had, of a tendency toward lethargy or of an unusually uneventful life or, as Swinburne had, of a talent much stronger in making "music" than in construction. Yeats works out of a full storehouse. The great number of what I have called, for want of a more suitable term, free lyrics—poems of distinct and yet highly asymmetrical form which permits the prosody to follow the vision rather than imposes a versification rigidly upon the vision—convinces one of that. The great interest in cadence tells the same story (though, as we have seen, not that story alone). And so does the persistence of a small handful of fixed forms —the quatrain, the octave, the sestet, and the tetrameter couplet—to which Yeats returns repeatedly. Yeats is more of a craftsman, more of a literary artist, than, say, Henry Vaughan or D. H. Lawrence; yet he belongs with Vaughan and Lawrence rather than with Poe, Dobson, or Swinburne. What Ruth Wallerstein has said of Vaughan may also be said, with little less accuracy, of Yeats : his "constructive gift seems . . . largely the by-product of general vision."[40]

Almost all of Yeats's poems, early and late alike, and whatever the measure or stanza, give an impression of color and firmness. Typically there is a singing or chanting effect; almost never is there anything like the lassitude that comes into so much of the verse of Arthur Symons or Oscar Wilde. Someone has spoken of Yeats (more to make a point than to disparage) as having an arrogant rhetoric; a part of that is an arrogant—I would rather say confident or challenging—prosody. Even when, as in so many of the later poems, he takes great pains to be loose and colloquial, there is almost always the firming confidence of intellectual power, of rich experience, of sensitive discrimination—and there is nearly always the color of rhyme. In short, Yeats's prosody is a lively and affirmative one; it is a direct reflection of his conviction that a poet must affirm life or give up hope of greatness. The making of a well-wrought stanza is a difficult delight : sensitive, arduous composition is a challenging, tonic, and ultimately pleasurable engagement; so that a bleakly pessimistic or nihilistic or self-pitying or lassitudinous octave or quatrain is a contradiction in terms : such a poem is immoral, not so much because of any enervating effect it might have on the society that reads it, but because it is hypocritical, false to the state of mind that produced it. Yeats is not an easy optimist; he took the tragic view of life: in the end he says yea and, like Wyndham Lewis, has nothing but scorn for modern softness and modern surrender to drabness, apathy, or hysteria.

All but a very few of the poems are in rhymed accentual-syllabic verse. In searching for the subtler reasons behind this constant choice, one should not overlook the obvious ones, and one of the most obvious is that the romantic Yeats shared the classical and Renaissance assumption that art is not life, that finished material is not raw material and is not inferior to it. The adolescent's or misguided romantic's urge is to unburden himself at any cost; the genuine artist's urge is to build and to create harmony. Accident and profusion, mere self-indulgence and self-therapy—the artist moves away, by instinct, from all that. He would construct intelligible and suasive form, he would delight in otherness and mutuality, in the fruits of empathy and surrender of the ego. The building of the artifact, the architectonic of matter and medium, is his first love, his *sine qua non* as an artist. The greater the number of elements one decides to control, the more the challenge; the deeper the engagement, the greater the final satisfaction. And in accentual-syllabic verse one must control elements that are more or less indeterminate in either purely accentual or purely syllabic verse (or of course in free verse); and to add rhyme is to add still another exigency. In its broadest outlines, then, Yeats's metrics is the concomitant of his passion for artistic control and of his fascination with challenge, discipline, responsibility.

His devotion to iambic and trochaic verse reveals the steady strength of his ambition to dine "at journey's end/With Landor and with Donne." The iambic and trochaic measures are, for modern English poets, the only serious ones in the accentual-syllabic repertoire. And this devotion reveals also Yeats's constant urge to dramatize his experience, to root the Great Commonplace in compelling particulars : English tri-syllabic meters are overrhythmical and exotic. In English, as in many other languages, iambic is the meter that seems least far removed from speech, and it is the meter that may be most easily loosened to accommodate actual speech cadences.

Yeats's attraction to linguistic vigor and freedom and his growing fondness for the realism and informality of the spoken language help explain, also, his pronounced interest in trochaic verse. Verse that alternates iambic and trochaic lines and that alternates them irregularly permits wide liberties and in itself creates or may easily be made to create something of the un-planned and intimate quality of speech. Yeats's frequent and relatively early iambic-trochaic couplet poems show him already on the way to the freedoms of some of the late poetry. The subject matter of most of the dominantly or purely tro-chaic poems shows us that Yeats found in the greatly emphatic quality of catalectic trochaic verse a form congenial to aphor-istic and incantatory expression.

The *ottava rima* seems to represent a fulfillment of Yeats's desire for wholeness through opposites : in it are reconciled his traditionalist and innovative impulses. The *ottava* is a traditional form in Western, but not in English, poetry. It grows organically out of Yeats's quatrains; still, it is not merely a double quatrain, but something new. It is a formal and elaborate stanza in itself, but Yeats counterpoints this quality with strong feeling and simple diction and speech locutions. Like the sestets and the other octaves, the *ottava* reflects the needs of the poet's mellow years : it provides room for sophisticated development of theme and effect; and it allows a fusion of both lyric and gnomic qualities. And it warns us, as Wallace Stevens's blank verse and John Fandel's and J. V. Cunningham's rhyming iambic trimeters warn us, not to be narrowly conclusive about the desuetude or obsoleteness of traditional forms.

The persistence of rhyme and the scarcity of blank verse (in the poems) emphasize the continuity of Yeats's development and show us that he recognized the advantages of staying with a feature which was as easy for him as alliteration was for Tennyson and which he had perfected. His love of rhyme places him within the mainstream of English lyric poetry and reveals his traditionalism once again. It aligns him with cultural and temperamental, and even to some extent with political, conservatism. Yeats himself came to think of his rhyme (and his meter) as a standard proudly displayed: a heroic mark of color and firmness thrust into the gray, joyless, inchoate face of modernism. The continuing rhyme also shows his determination to remain a lyrical and imaginative writer rather than to become a maker of the well-made play or of the judicious philosophical poem. The ordering and formalizing characteristics of rhyme and the intricacies of turn and return it invites allow us to see still another manifestation of Yeats's love of order and ritual. And without question Yeats's rhyme is often a correlative of his love of musical and marmoreal beauty, a love the realism of his later years tempered but never destroyed. His slant rhyme is a way out of rhyming difficulties, a relief to his ear, and sometimes an onomatopoeia of the "lust and rage" that invited his late muse into muted and sometimes consciously dissonant song. His exploitation of it extends our knowledge of its capabilities and has undoubtedly given impetus to the increasing use of it we have witnessed in the past few decades.

Rhyme is one way of identifying the line, an instrument peculiar to poetry. There are two other prosodic line-marking devices at the poet's disposal—end-pause and avoidance of light terminations—and Yeats utilizes them consistently. His devotion to them shows him to be clearly on the side of the artists. A poem should not sprawl and stagger like nascent thought or completely extempore speech; it should preserve some measure of naturalness but still sing or chant or fall elegantly; in short, it should be sensitive and incantatory. Not sharing our egalitarian bias, Yeats saw aesthetic distance as neither antisocial nor antipoetic. Typically his lines are not only rhymed but end-paused on strong stresses. Consequently even when the diction is colloquial and the meter somewhat faint and irregular, the poems are always quite unlike talk or prose. The strength of Yeats's lines is a paradox, of course: it follows from, and reconciles, opposites: the man's vigor and passionateness as well as the artist's aesthetic sensibility.

The metrical irregularity and the cadence lines and poems of his later years place him in the good company of many English masters. It is the artist muting his art and extending his freedom—not without peril, of course. It is the final extension of Yeats's desire for a prosody that could suggest the passionate or spontaneous voice without surrendering consummate artistry and that would be able to yield at every point to sense and to indispensable word. It is the poet who has decided to be inclusive, to welcome alike his realist impulses and his vision of supernature, to include with his song convivial talk and the public man's accent. The achievement of this prosody reflects, in Richard Ellmann's word, "the abandon to which old age entitled him, and the control which a lifetime of painful development had made habitual."[41]

The organic development of Yeats's art of verse would seem to argue for greater self-knowledge and moral firmness than certain critics (Yvor Winters, for example) have been willing to credit him with. Moral laxity, so the argument goes, may well express itself in metrical laxity. Absence of a code may produce absence of meter; or a code loosely held may feel most congenial in loose meter. Now, I happen to agree with those critics who see an element of moral enervation and relativism in that gradual loosening and abandonment of our traditional and determinate verse forms which has been the history of recent English poetry. One way the old certainties and optimisms expressed themselves, I myself feel sure, was in certainty or firmness of metrics (once such firmness had been made available, as by Chaucer and then again by Surrey and Sackville). For a world that believes in a benevolent God, a harmonious universe, and a revealed morality, a couplet or a sonnet, not a run of *vers libre,* is the better paradigm. Free verse and forms very close to it begin to appear in the age of Arnold, the age that felt the last coherence go, under the impacts of technological isolation and ennui, of Darwinism, Marxist determinism, and the Higher Criticism. But surely no necessary correlation exists. A host of other causes may lie behind a poet's moving away from metrical fixity : for example, curiosity about new metrical possibilities, a sense of confinement or fatigue, or a desire for a less idealized idiom. Shakespearean blank verse is looser than Marlovian, but no one can be found, I think, who will give the moral palm to Kit Marlowe. Shakespeare's measure itself shows a progressive taste for freedom. Is the poet of *Antony and Cleopatra* and *The Tempest* more suspect than the poet of *Romeo and Juliet?* Is there evidence of moral confusion in the liberated measure of Bridges's late *Testament of Beauty* that is not present in the Laureate's early meticulous rhyming verse?

Long ago T. S. Eliot pointed out that Yeats is one of those poets who are best understood and best appreciated when their poems are read against one another and read in the light of some knowledge of the poet's life. Many of the Irish poet's attitudes and interests and beliefs, many aspects of his spirit, have remained puzzling and have generated widely different interpretations; any and all new evidence is therefore worth getting at. And so I have tried to see what image the prosody itself reflects. Still, I would like to remind the reader that my chief purpose in this book has been to describe Yeats's metrical art and to discover the rationale of his choice. Personality is ultimately translated into the uniqueness and independence of individual poems. The impact of a work of art should not, and ultimately dare not, depend upon our knowledge of the life and personality of the artist who constructed it. Poetry that survives does so, not because it leads us back to the particularities of the man who wrote it, but because it has transcended those details; the man is obscure and two fifths undistinguished and two fifths foolish; it is in the remaining fifth that he triumphs : the poem is translucent and perfected. It is not the soul of Yeats that one seeks, but the beauty, knowledge, and power in his art.

Notes

The texts of all the poems from which I have quoted are, unless otherwise specified, those of the 1956 edition of *The Collected Poems of W. B. Yeats* and of the 1953 edition of *The Collected Plays of W. B. Yeats.* Parenthetical dates following the title of a work refer to the year of publication.

[1] Of course, we should be careful not to make too much of the distinction between the historical and the personal: history being after all, only the sums of individual actions. A period's distinctive aesthetic preferences—in prosody, no less than in fiction, fashion, or furniture—are nothing more than a general consent, a common ground among individuals. Thus to take what seems a clear instance, Crabbe's choice of the heroic couplet is "historical": like other poets of his day, he is likely to choose it (or its approved rival, blank verse) simply because it is familiar and illustrious. But it is also a personal choice: free, after all, to choose some other form, Crabbe acquiesces in the main fashion, and not necessarily out of conscious deference or unconscious inheritance but as well, perhaps, because he judged the pentameter couplet a form eminently suited to his particular needs and talent.

[2] In *A Vision,* and earlier, Yeats sought to account for such "antithetical dream." His explanation is not always clear, but in cases like those of Morris and Landor, at least, a part of it will reduce to a very sensible statement: men of higher nature are likely to be impatient of their own limitations and imperfections, and consequently to seek freedom and wholeness—unity of being, in Yeats's phrase—by admiring and embracing the qualities they themselves lack. In a single sentence in *Per Amica Silentia Lunae* (p. 16) Yeats crystallizes his whole understanding of the "anti-selves" of Landor and Morris: "William Morris, a happy, busy, most irascible man, described dim colour and pensive emotion, following, beyond any man of his time, an indolent Muse; while Savage Landor topped us all in calm nobility when the pen was in his hand, as in the daily violence of his passion when he had laid it down."

[3] If one were asked what, besides the need to make a living and the itch to make a mark, was the main force behind the writing of Shakespeare's plays, one could do worse than answer, "blank verse."

Once Marlowe arrived on the scene, the poets of Albion were absolutely enchanted with this new five-stop instrument, and they played it for all it was worth. The wit who remarked that Plato and pentameter made the English poetic renaissance had not far to go toward the truth. Thanks to a metrical experiment commenced by Surrey and continued by Marlowe, we have *King Lear*. Unrhyming ta-TUM ta-TUM ta-TUM ta-TUM ta-TUM as a kind of cantus firmus around which variations could be worked was novel, and fairly easy, and proved to be delightful on the stage. If the Lear legend had not existed for Shakespeare to get his hands on, then some other story—there being in his day an abundance of suitable tales yet untouched or only poorly assimilated by the stage—would have served; but Shakespeare without blank verse is inconceivable. The popular notion—assumed also by some "history of ideas" and "archetypal pattern" critics, most of whom have never thought of prosody except to think it beneath contempt —is that literary works are always brought into being by plots and ideas. The fact is that imaginative literature is often inspired by the desire to pay court to a genre or manner, or even to try out a promising new beat or stanza that has caught one's attention. Genre often, and perhaps as a rule, precedes conception. Verse satire, a man of a certain temperament discovers, is delightful; to become a verse satirist would be a fine thing. The tone, the manner, the texture, is exhilarating; the thing satirized is often a secondary consideration. It was not exactly Spenser's Platonism, or his Protestantism or his six virtues, that bred the seventeenth-century Spenserians; it was Spenserian texture. What is the novice American poet's chief inspiration at present? (One is almost afraid to ask.) It is the manner, the tone and rhythm, of William Carlos Williams or Charles Olson or Dylan Thomas. It is a key, a tonality, a distinctive pattern, that sets the young artist afire; any subject or imagined situation that enables him to reproduce it, or something like it but still his own, will do. Of course ideas and "dominant images" are beginning to form in the young man's head; but they do not form in a toneless, disembodied way. The more of a true artist (if only in potential) he is, the less will he be able to, or want to, separate the plots and ideas he encounters from the textures in which they have come to him. A poet reads Plato (or Jowett-Plato), not the abstraction "Platonic philosophy." Of course it may be to some degree the *Weltanschauung* that so fascinates the young writer. But where does he see that? It is incarnated, particularized in the medium, in the specifics of tone, rhythm, image, structure. Because he falls in love with a tune, a genre, a manner, a prosody, the poet will search out a subject that makes them possible.

4   *Autobiographies* (New York: Macmillan, 1927), p. 392.

5   Richard Ellman, *Yeats, the Man and the Masks* (New York: Macmillan, 1948), p. 140.

6   *The Southern Review: W. B. Yeats Memorial Issue,* VII: 3 (1941), 661.

7   Thomas Parkinson, *W. B. Yeats, Self-Critic* (Berkeley: University of California Press, 1951).

8   Donald A. Stauffer, *The Golden Nightingale* (New York: Macmillan, 1949), p. 17.

9   *Ideas of Good and Evil* (New York: Macmillan, 1903), p. 91.

10 Yeats's reverence for "traditional" English poetry (and his interpretation of himself as belonging squarely within that tradition) is of course expressed in many places in his essays, letters, and poems, but nowhere more clearly or eloquently than in a letter to Dorothy Wellesley postmarked April 20, 1936. The text of the letter is available in Allan Wade's collection *The Letters of W. B. Yeats* (New York: Macmillan, 1955), p. 852. In subsequent references I shall call this book simply *Letters.*

11 My count. The figure includes sections of poems, if the sections themselves constitute, in actuality, independent or relatively independent poems. Such inclusion is open to objection, but as there are only a very few such cases, the matter is of no great consequence one way or the other. Also, it may be objected that my analysis should proceed in terms of the total body of Yeats's poems —the suppressed poems (to be found in the Allt & Alspach *Variorum*) as well as the authorized ones. But in this case the uncollected or suppressed poems—all juvenilia—represent the level of mere speech, not the level of final choice, where personality at last finds itself and shows itself.

12 Yeats's avoidance of classical and of the usual French imitations is not to be explained simply by the fact that he never learned any language but English. Many English poets whose knowledge of other tongues has been slight have tried their hands at such models: they have followed the forms as these have already been adapted by other English poets, or they have been able to learn the formal pattern without really learning the language itself (as it is easier to scan Vergil than to translate him).

13 For excellent detailed studies of Yeats's habits of composition, the reader should consult Jon Stallworthy's *Between the Lines: Yeats's Poetry in the Making* (Oxford: Clarendon Press, 1963) and Thomas Parkinson's *W. B. Yeats: The Later Poetry* (Berkeley: University of California Press, 1964).

14 Many of the later poems, though not presented typographically as quatrains, use the quatrain pattern and could, in many cases without much or any aesthetic injury, be printed on the page as

individual quatrains. "Politics," "Mohini Chatterjee," and "Death," for example.

15 Joseph Hone, *W. B. Yeats* (New York: Macmillan, 1942), p. 489.

16 Ibid., p. 47.

17 Ibid., p. 47. The letter, dated August 19, 1937, is printed in *Letters*, p. 896.

18 *Letters on Poetry from W. B. Yeats to Dorothy Wellesley* (London & New York: Oxford University Press, 1940), p. 5.

19 Hone, p. 489.

20 *The Autobiography of William Butler Yeats* (New York: Macmillan, 1953), p. 63.

21 Ibid., p. 76.

22 For a cogent discussion of trisyllabic measures, see Paul Fussell, Jr., *Poetic Meter and Poetic Form* (New York: Random House, 1965).

23 *Essays and Introductions*, p. 524.

24 There is not yet and, considering the notorious temperament of prosodists, there probably never will be, general agreement about what the traditional seven-syllable English line should be called. It has been termed "trochaic" or "truncated iambic" or "septa-syllabic" as one pleases. "Truncated iambic" may be more accurate (the seven-syllable line is normally found as a variant in what is basically an iambic tetrameter couplet poem); but "trochaic" is more familiar and is more manageable in writing as in speaking. Terminological difficulties should not be allowed to impede essential understanding. No matter what one calls the line, or how one notates the scansion, its rhythmical quality is certainly not the same as that of ordinary iambic meter. The line is best seen, I think, as rendering an effect of tension: on the one hand, there is the sense that the trochaic unit (or "rising rhythm") is the norm; on the other, there is our English tendency to slip into good old iambic whenever it is possible to do so.

25 In the 1953 *Autobiography* (p. 76) he says, "I wanted the strongest passions, passions that had nothing to do with observation." In a letter to Dorothy Wellesley dated December 21, 1935 (*Letters*, p. 845) he says, "I shall not use 'sprung verse' . . . I dislike the constant uncertainty as to where the accent falls; it seems to make the verse vague and weak. I like a strong driving force." Many similar remarks could be quoted.

26 Thomas Parkinson, *W. B. Yeats, Self-Critic*, pp. 138–45.

27 The eleventh line is not thus repeated in the earliest printed versions of the poem (i.e., in the *Dublin University Review* of October, 1885, and in *The Wanderings of Oisin and Other Poems*, 1889). The revision was made, however, as early as 1895 for *Poems*.

28 Henry Lanz, *The Physical Basis of Rime* (Stanford, 1931). This profound, thorough, and wonderfully readable work of the most painstaking scholarship is all but unknown today. I must here express my indebtedness to it and to Dr. Francis Lee Utley, who many years ago directed me to it.

29 Yeats was of course more reactionary in theory than in practice, as his "liberal" voting record in the Irish Senate testifies. His politics is an extremely complicated matter. The best extended discussion of it so far is Conor Cruise O'Brien's essay "Passion and Cunning: An Essay on the Politics of W. B. Yeats" in the centenary volume *In Excited Reverie*, edited by A. Norman Jeffares and K. G. W. Cross (London: Macmillan, 1965). The last word, however, has by no means been said, and there is little hope of its being said until some scholar other than one of the Left takes up the subject. Yeats's distance from fascism and other modern "isms," and his political reasonableness, are well articulated in a letter to Ethel Mannin dated November, 30, 1936 (*Letters*, p. 869). His ultimate disenchantment with all modern politics is clearly expressed in his letters to Ethel Mannin; see, for example, the letter to her postmarked February 11, 1937 (*Letters*, p. 881).

30 *Letters*, p. 583.

31 *Essays and Introductions*, p. 521.

32 Of course it is possible to scan "That his hair is beautiful" as trochaic meter. But that is an afterthought; the ear does not perceive any trochaic beat here, perhaps because there is none elsewhere in these lines, and because there is such a naturalness and simplicity about the expression.

33 *Essays and Introductions*, p. 522.

34 Ibid., p. 524.

35 Sir Herbert Grierson's incredulity, expressed in his introduction to V. K. N. Menon's book, *The Development of William Butler Yeats* (Edinburgh: Oliver and Boyd, 1942), about Yeats's alleged fascist inclinations, is a valuable corrective to Menon's, and others', anxiety. A sane, if summary, discussion of Yeats's politics and a similar skepticism about his supposed fascism will be found in Arland Ussher's *Three Great Irishmen* (New York: New American Library of World Literature, 1957), pp. 70-4. In a· quite recent essay (see Note 29) Conor Cruise O'Brien also concludes that Yeats is best thought of as an aristocrat, not as a fascist.

36 Robert Bridges, *Milton's Prosody* (Oxford: Oxford University Press, 1921), p. 51.

37 The fifteen poems written wholly or partly in *ottava rima:*
"Sailing to Byzantium," *The Tower*, 1928.
"Meditations in Time of Civil War" (Parts I, IV), *The Tower*.

"Nineteen Hundred and Nineteen" (Part I), *The Tower*.
"Among School Children," *The Tower*.
"Coole Park, 1929," *The Winding Stair and Other Poems*, 1933.
"Coole Park and Ballylee," *The Winding Stair and Other Poems*.
"Veronica's Napkin," *The Winding Stair and Other Poems*.
"The Choice," *The Winding Stair and Other Poems*.
"Vacillation" (Parts II, III), *The Winding Stair and Other Poems*.
"A Woman Young and Old" (Part VIII), *The Winding Stair and Other Poems*.
"Parnell's Funeral" (Part I), *A Full Moon in March*, 1935.
"The Gyres," *Last Poems*, 1936-39.
"The Municipal Gallery Revisited," *Last Poems*.
"The Statues," *Last Poems*.
"The Circus Animals' Desertion," *Last Poems*.

[38] *W. B. Yeats: the Later Poetry*, p. 199.

[39] In Yeats's first five books of poems (up to, but not including, *The Wild Swans at Coole*) there are fourteen octave poems; in his last six books there are forty-eight. Following is a tabulation of Yeats's verse forms as they appear in the authorized *Collected Poems:*

Couplets	49
Triplets	6
Tercets	2
Terza Rima	1
Quatrains	126
Pentains	16
Sestets	63
Septains	11
Rhyme Royals	2
Octaves	62
9-line stanzas	2
10-line stanzas	11
11-line stanzas	2
12-line stanzas	1
13-line stanzas	1
14-line stanzas	1
Sonnets	4
Blank Verse	13
Accentual Hexameter	1
Choric (Irregular)	3
Irregular Rhyming	13
	390

Quatrains, sestets, and octaves account for nearly two-thirds of

Yeats's poems. In the first six books there are 70 quatrain poems; in the last six books (which contain many more poems) there are 56. No pentameter octaves at all appear in the last six books. Sestets are similarly infrequent in the first six books (8) and ubiquitous in the last six (55). All but a few of the sestets have one of the following rhyme schemes: *xaxaxa, ababcc, xaxabb, abcabc.*

The direction is distinct. The quatrain continues to be a favorite form. Yeats has mastered it too well to abandon it. And yet it does fall off, and the larger sestets and octaves increase. Yeats needs more room and wants more urgently the intensity, the incisiveness, and the incantatory qualities of the couplets and repeated rhymes available in both the sestets and octaves.

A number of Yeats's poems, particularly the later ones, are divided into sections; in many cases these sections, closely related as they are, also constitute in some ways independent poems. I have included such sections in my count, so that my total of 390 is slightly greater than the total number of poems in the twelve books of the *Collected Poems.* However, if all the sections of a sectioned poem use the same verse form, I count the form only once.

I must point out, too, that in a few cases it is possible to quarrel with my classification: sometimes it is difficult to say whether a poem should be classed as an octave or as two linked quatrains, and whether a stanza of four lines with a two-line refrain should be considered a quatrain or a sestet. Fortunately there are not enough such cases to invalidate the proportions of the figures given above.

[40] Ruth Wallerstein, *Studies in Seventeenth Century Poetic* (Madison: University of Wisconsin Press, 1950), p. 155.

[41] Richard Ellmann, *The Identity of Yeats* (New York: Macmillan, 1954), p. 180.